# Web Sites That Work

# ROGER BLACK

# WEB SITES THAT WORK

## WITH SEAN ELDER

**Adobe Press**
**San Jose, California**

Library of Congress Catalog No.: 96-78988

ISBN: 1-56830-346-7

10 9 8 7 6 5 4 3 2 First Printing: February 1997

The information in this book is furnished for informational use only, is subject to change without notice, and should not be construed as a commitment by Adobe Systems Incorporated. Adobe Systems Incorporated assumes no responsibility for any errors or inaccuracies that may appear in this book. The software mentioned in this book is furnished under license and may only be used or copied in accordance with the terms of such license. Contact the software manufacturer directly for terms of software licenses for any software mentioned in this book not originating from Adobe Systems Incorporated.

Adobe, the Adobe Press logo, Acrobat, Adobe Illustrator, Adobe After Effects, Adobe PageMill, Adobe PageMaker, Adobe Photoshop, Adobe SiteMill, and Postscript are trademarks of Adobe Systems Incorporated. All other brand or product names are the trademarks or registered trademarks of their respective holders.

Printed in the United States of America by GAC Shepard Poorman, Indianapolis, Indiana. Published simultaneously in Canada.

Adobe Press books are published and distributed by Macmillan Computer Publishing USA. For individual, educational, corporate, or retail sales accounts, call 1-800-428-5331, or 317-581-3500. For information address Macmillan Computer Publishing USA, 201 West 103rd Street, Indianapolis, IN 46290, or at http://www.mcp.com.

**Photographs of Roger Black on the cover and on pages 2, 3, 18-19, 42-43, 84, 115, 130, 178-179, 186-187, and 240 are © Andy Freeburg, 1997.**

**Photographs of the Interactive Bureau Offices on pages 8, 150, 161, 164, 167, and 170 are © John Hall, 1997.**

**Edited and designed by Tom Morgan and John Miller**
**Special thanks to Patrick Ames**

**W**hen Patrick Ames, the Publisher of Adobe Press, suggested this book, it was clear that it would be a lot better (and might actually be on time) if I approached it like a design project. John Miller and Tom Morgan of Interactive Bureau's San Francisco office were at that first meeting, and they agreed to manage the project from the start. It was clear that we would need a lot of help. For one thing, none of us is a writer by trade. Sean Elder agreed and conducted the research and interviews as well.

John and Tom designed it. And everyone at Interactive Bureau in New York, Monterrey, Paris and Barcelona got involved, at least to contribute a quote or a fact or a jpeg file. Even the print studios (my partners in those cities and elsewhere) got roped in, because we wanted to show that lessons we learned designing magazines and newspapers were useful on the Internet.

Finally, it became clear that it would be crazy to put the whole thing in the first person. "I" this, and "I" that. For one thing, the work on the book has been collaborative, as have all the design projects. So, after this page, no more me. It's us, our colleagues, and our clients.

I am grateful to all of them—for this book, for all the designs in it, and for all the work to come.

**—Roger Black**

# Contents

Above, Esquire magazine, 1991. Left, @Home home page, 1996.

# Introduction

# Introduction

Interactive Bureau

*Design is the answer.*
*What was the question, again?*

The Internet is a question. The answer is being formulated now by programmers, producers, editors, content providers, sysops, Webmeisters, users, visitors, Web watchers, cable operators, phone companies, and designers. Especially designers.

Web sites are even more dependent on good design than print is. After all, even a magazine with minimum design (take *The Nation*) gets its information across. You buy it because you care about the issues in its headlines. If you want more, jump inside. Print on paper. Hold it in your hands. Recycle when finished.

But Web sites are visual: one screen at a time. Encouraging the viewer to find what is beneath that first layer—even learn that there is more—is a problem for designers. It is their job to take the user-browser-viewer-reader through the Dance of the Seven (or Seven Thousands) Veils. The designer's job is to be barker and stripper, for the main show and side. It is not enough to get people through the front door, to your home page. You have to bring them inside and, once they are in, try not to confuse or frustrate them. You must entertain and inform them and allow them to jump from one thing to the next with the greatest of ease. Otherwise they don't come back, and the circus folds its tents, and all the acrobats, jugglers, and clowns go back to their day jobs.

Fuse, Neville Brody's quarterly of experimental type faces.

Web sites that work are sites that do what you want to do. They don't insult your intelligence, but neither do they obfuscate. They must indicate the wealth of material that lies behind that first screen, but also allow you options and alternate means of approach. It is no wonder that search engines like Yahoo! have made money while so many Web sites have failed: the compass is worth more than the land.

The answer may lie in better selling the land—in urban planning, if you will. The solution to timeless Internet problems—navigation, access to information—will be provided by design. Good design means pertinent information. Good design means content. Good design means good surfing, exploring, gathering. The designer, then, is the Web's real pathfinder. The medium's hopes rest on their shoulders, for if they don't succeed, how will the wonders of the Web survive? Design is the answer.

What was the question, again?

"The Internet is an enormous, unresolved composite," says Roger Black. "And we aren't. We have backgrounds in, say, print. Or software. You can find people that have experience in two of the converging industries—there are magazine editors who have put out Web sites—but finding people that know three is a lot harder. Where are the magazine editors that have done Web sites and TV shows?

"At times you hear someone express great satisfaction with what they've done on the Net. But take another look. It's very likely that they're

# Pigs, *dudes,* slimeballs, *victims,* studs, *wimps,* girl toys, *fools,* heroes, human beings?

[Author of *The Beauty Myth*]
NAOMI WOLF

With festive abandon, men have been reaping the spoils of the women's movement and its sexual revolution—but have been unwilling as they partied to pay their debts to either.

[Author of *Geek Love*]
KATHERINE DUNN

It's damage-assessment time. Like generals, women are wondering what condition the enemy is in after twenty several years of bombardment with the idea that every wrong and vile thing that ever happened on the planet is their fault: the results

ESQUIRE·OCTOBER 1991     156     OCTOBER 1991·ESQUIRE 137

Rhonda Rubenstein's design for Esquire magazine, 1991.

INTRODUCTION

For someone who started in print, the most alarming thing about the Internet is that the reader can publish. It takes a while to remember that we are not broadcasting from on high.

happy because the result reminds them of 'home.'

"So the magazine art director makes Web pages that look like *Time*. Computer geeks make pages resembling homework. Ad guys churn out baseball stadium banners. And phone people are hooking up networks.

"The fact is we're not there yet. We don't really know what the Internet is. It's too big: the Internet is simply the conduit for all information and entertainment, since all of it is rapidly being digitized. And, so despite the land rush, there is lots of room to pitch a stake and plenty of time to get in and get it right.

"For someone like me, who started in print, the most alarming thing about the Internet is that the reader can publish. It takes a while to remember that we are not broadcasting from on high, we are not delivering typeset, printed pieces. The Net is a space where the reader actually writes.

"It's necessary to move from a linear, one-way paradigm, like newspapers, to a two-way paradigm—like telephones. On the Net, information isn't tumbling down a hierarchy; it's flowing collaboratively. Designers have to move aside and make a place where the customer can speak, where they're comfortable and feel at home. It's fascinating; this is a very challenging design space."

In the seventies and eighties, Roger Black became one of the most influential designers in the magazine and newspaper world. As art director of the *New York Times* and *Rolling Stone* (which received the National Magazine Award for Design during his tenure), Black developed an immediately identifiable style: sparse, clean layouts, a strong use of classic serif and slab serif fonts, a style that made editorial its priority. During this period, *Newsweek*, *Esquire*, *Foreign Affairs* and *Ad Age*, were redesigned by Black.

"*Rolling Stone* influenced a lot of people working in design," says John Schmitz, who has worked with

Roger Black was art director of Rolling Stone from 1975 to 1979. At right, dug from the vaults, is designer Mary Robertson's original paste-up for the "Rock and Roll" section.

# ROCK and ROLL

## Addio, monti sorgenti dall

E La Fatica genera sempre la Scienza e l'Ozio genera Schiller était un homme d'un génie rare et d'une bonne foi parfaite; ces deux qualités de-

stage figure Peter Gabriel quit Genesis last May, many thought that the band was in serious trouble. Now, with a new album, *A Trick of the Tail*, and a North American tour which began in Toronto on March 31st, the band members and Gabriel agree that everything's going well.

After Gabriel announced his decision, some 400 applicants auditioned to replace him. Eventually it became apparent that the best successor was already in the band.

"It was very frustrating," Genesis drummer Phil Collins recalled. "I was singing and teaching them, and none of them were coming up to scratch. We even

### Schiller était un

At the encouragement of his wife, Collins then suggested that he should do the band's onstage singing. The idea was immediately dismissed, but two months later, with no sign of another lead singer, guitarists Mike Rutherford and Steve Hackett and keyboard player Tony Banks agreed—as long as another drummer could be found. Former Yes and King Crimson member Bill Bruford was drafted as a guest touring member, went in to record the album without a singer. I was down to sing a couple of acoustic songs. As far as the heavier songs went, I was an unknown quantity.

"It came to the point where we had to do 'Squonk' [the album's most Zeppelin-like cut] and I had a go. Obviously it went okay, so we went through the rest of the album. At that point we felt very confident. We knew as a four-

of the group staying around to offer encouragement.

Gabriel's departure did cause some difficulties. "Lyric writing was more of a challenge 'cause we didn't have a very individual style, and Gabriel had been entirely responsible for the humor within the band," Collins said. "Otherwise, the material was put together much as before—sitting around the rehearsal room having the odd pieces of material and later on gluing them together." Gabriel's elaborate mime routines also seem to be a thing of the past. "The actual visual presentation of the stage will be the same as before, but more refined," Collins said about the forthcoming tour. "We'll be using movies as well as slides. There'll be a few special effects. We won't be using dry ice. I won't be wearing costumes."

What does Gabriel think of all this? In New York to talk to producer Bob Ezrin and search for a U.S. label (he's signed to Charisma in England), Gabriel said that he'd heard and liked *A Trick of the Tail*—"quite a lot. A few

### RIFORMA

Black in print and online. "The atmosphere was different then, but it's similar to David Carson's influence today. Actually, Black's work may have been even more influential, because there really wasn't as much good graphic design around."

As a pioneer in desktop publishing, Black was a natural candidate for the Internet. In 1994, in response to client demand and his own growing interest, Black cofounded (with David Berlow and Jock Spivy) the Interactive Bureau. With such early successes as the Discovery Channel Online and USA Today, the IAB made its presence felt on the Web. And though its form is still being defined by people from varied disciplines—telecommunications, television, cable, movies, advertising, magazines electronics, and newspapers—its culture was one suspicious of leaders and visionaries, of anyone who professed to have The Answer.

"I think we got a jump on a lot of people partly because of our print experience and because of Roger's broad-reaching interest in a lot of ideas and content-type media," says Schmitz, who is now vice president of design at IAB. "But also in terms of the hands-on experience we had, in terms of putting things together in the early days with Discovery and USA Today, we learned a lot. We came up against some heavy-duty brick walls where we realized, Oh hell, you can't do that, can you?"

If there are walls in Web design, in the World Wide Web itself—then it is the designer's job to find the doors, light the path, and even turn on the exit signs. Like Harold with his purple crayon, the designer must draw what is needed. Got an ocean? Draw yourself a boat. Can't find your way home? Draw a window around the moon and suddenly you're back in your room.

But don't tell the user what to do. Don't tell him how to sail the boat

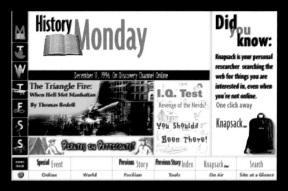

Home pages for the Discovery Channel Online, designed by Jessica Helfand, and USA Today, designed by John Schmitz.

Origianl sketches for the new
format of Newsweek, 1985.

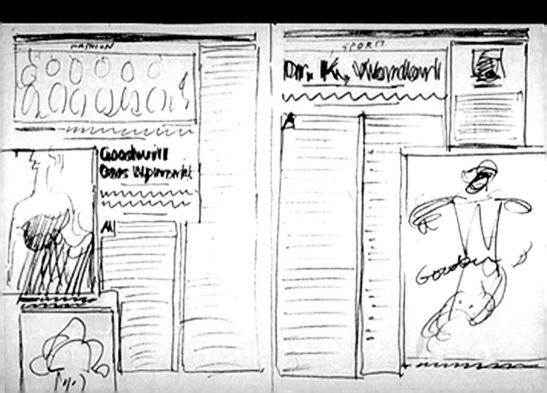

or, if it needs an outboard, don't tell her how to drive.

"One thing to learn is this: the *Don't Click Here* button is the one that everybody will click," says Black. "People want to do what they're not supposed to. In fact, the typical relationship between provider and consumer is the consumer trying to break the rules, to circumvent the imposed structure. We fast-forward to the end of the movie, and read magazines from the back.

"With the Internet there are no longer providers and customers, or publishers and readers. The new order makes the viewer the producer, the director, the editor. It's a collaboration. A designer can put a button on a page. But he can't tell 'em where to click."

# Rules That Work

*A Design Primer*

# Rules That Work

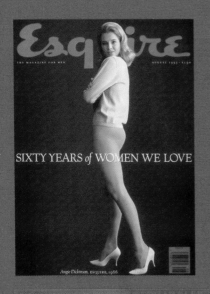

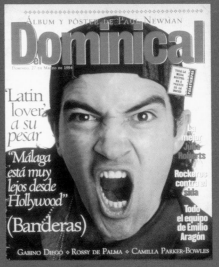

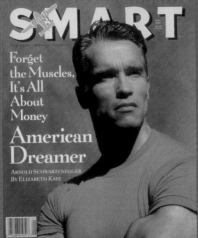

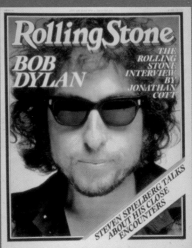

**Rule No. 7**

The Interactive Bureau site outlines Black's theories of Internet design. It also gives examples of the good, the bad, and the ugly. (www.iab.com)

When it comes to the Web, some would say rules were made to be broken. Though chaos has its place in physics and cosmology, one need only traverse the endless morass of the World Wide Web —empty skyscrapers, abandoned theme parks, murky dens broken up by the occasional clean, well-lighted place—to see that there is something that separates Web sites that work from dead air.

Where does good Web design come from? Black believes the principles that have informed quality print design for hundreds of years are equally valid online; in some cases, they are even more so. Here, then, are …

## The Ten Rules of Design

# 1.

### Put content on every page.

Design shouldn't be mere decoration; it must convey information. Or entertainment. The aging interface for America Online is a great example of what *not* to do. A reader should never have to plow through forests of buttons to get simple news. Content should come to the surface on every single level.

On the front page of a newspaper, you don't put a picture of Clinton shaking hands with Yeltsin; we've already seen that picture; it's lost all of its meaning. It's important to get down to the next level, to try to bring more content to the surface, to get more content out of the photograph that you put on your front page.

With Web sites, it's the same thing: trying to come up with something that doesn't look like something that has been completely stripped of its content. Everybody wants a nav bar that has a question mark for the help sign. The designer has to avoid useless and confusing icons.

**Corollary to Rule No. 1:** Nobody reads anything. At least not everything. The only person that will read every word of what you've written is your mother. Everybody else is too busy.

In magazines or in Web sites, people skim and surf. If you don't give them something quickly, they absorb nothing. So you have to make sure there's content on every page.

And make it easy to read. Most sites try to crowd too much onto a page—much better to break information down into smaller bits. This is not to suggest you always throw out text; just try to make it as accessible as possible.

MSNBC was worried about content. They have a lot of content; their problem is that they have stuff that people don't know about and don't know how to find. They were using an analogy of an iceberg in the ocean: there's all this stuff and the trick is trying to figure out a way to get access to it. But we looked at it like this: "It's the tip of the iceberg, but it's not in an ocean; it's in a cup of coffee. There's not room for it all! There are only so many directionals you can put on the page before it's overwhelmed, before the page looks full."

This is a problem Web designers constantly grapple with. There's all this content; if you want to make it easy to navigate, you can start whipping out maps and navigation bars that show where you are, but if you have 600 pages, it will look like the phone book. At some point, you have to make strong editorial choices about the hierarchies of information—and just make it simple and clear. You can't get all the information on the surface of that cup of coffee.

**—Tom Morgan, Interactive Bureau**

# Nobody Reads Anything

To get a simple stock quote in **AOL**, you have to click through four layers. No one has the patience to do this! Bring content to every level: IAB's early sketches for **MSNBC** take you to the story you want directly off the home page.

White, black, and red: The earliest printers got it.
The Gutenberg Bible, 1456.

I think people read the Web like they read a billboard when they're going down the freeway. If they don't get it pretty fast, they're going to run off the road. A lot of designers like very groovy Photoshop backgrounds, with lots of layers, and a word here, a word there that you click to. That's fine in a CD or in a magazine or a book. But on the Web, people are in a hurry. They don't really care about your dumb design. They want to get something. They want to find out things, they want information fast. That's still what the Web is about. It's probably going to be about that for a long, long time. If you want big, flowing images, go to TV. A lot of interactive designers are in denial about this.

**—John Schmitz, Interactive Bureau**

# 2,3,4.

**The first color is white.**
**The second color is black.**
**The third color is red.**

Calligraphers and early printers grasped this over 500 years ago, and experience has proved them exactly right.

In print, white is the absence of all color, while in video, it's every color firing at full strength. It is the brightest color; it should be used much more in design. And it's even more important on the Web. White is the best background.

Black holds the highest contrast to white, and so it is the first choice for type set on a white background. Yet we increasingly see—on the Web and in print—designers running amok and putting the type in yellow on an orange background, or worse. You can't read it; there's not enough contrast between the figure and the ground.

White, black, and red: Roger Black's design for the cover of the 10th anniversary issue of Rolling Stone, 1977.

# White, Black, and Red

**They're the best colors—striking, readable, in perfect contrast—and have been used since day one . . .**

Inca tapestry, circa 1490.

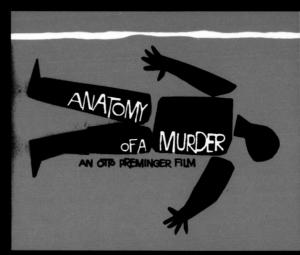

Saul Bass, 1961.

TALES
BY
TOLSTOY

ILLUSTRATED

The Folio Society, 1947.

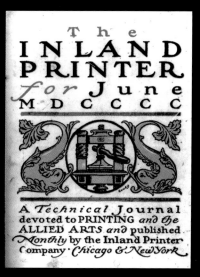

The Inland Printer, 1900.

Why do the designers do it? Because it's easy to do and they labor under the misconception that they must be novel. (Sorry, illegible design has been around for years.) *Wired* and HotWired are obvious examples of Design Before Legibility. For good readable use of black and white for text, look at *Foreign Affairs* magazine, or on the Web, www.suck.com.

(Hint: If you can't stand a white background, use a black background with white type. The worst that can happen is that people will think you support free speech on the Net.)

And then there is red. Yellow won't read against white; blue fades against black. But red is perfect. Red headlines sell magazines on newsstands twice as much as any other color. There are certain hardwired facts about human visual response that you'd be a fool to ignore. Like instinctive reactions to colors. Red is nature's danger color and is a great way to add accent to a black-and-white page. (Warning: Some colors of red work better than others against a black background.)

White, black, and red are the best. You've got to be very careful with other colors. We actually did a site, the FutureTense site, with all these autumn colors; they were dead set on this. They wanted it very nontechy. We had to work very hard to make this effective on the Web. It's much softer. It's a little more atmospheric in a different kind of way.

**—John Schmitz, Interactive Bureau**

# 5.

## Never letterspace lowercase.

When you do this, the natural, built-in rhythm of the letters is ruined. Despite the current trend in book jackets, this is simply not done. Frederic Goudy put it best: "A man who would letterspace lowercase would shag a sheep."

Basically, the theory is that spacing out lowercase type is appalling. It's wrong. And just because every book you pick up has a jacket design employing this doesn't mean it's okay. As Roger is fond of saying, "Wait five

# Eye Chart

**It's not as if it isn't hard enough to read on a monitor. So why make it harder?**

## GOOD CONTRAST

www.iab.com

www.suck.com

www.discovery.com

## NOT SO GOOD

www.wired.com

www.io360.com

www.word.com

RULES THAT WORK

# Letterspaced Lowercase!

To look at books these days, you'd

think it was sheer brilliance. But it's

a bad idea. It might look hip now, but

wait five years and look again.

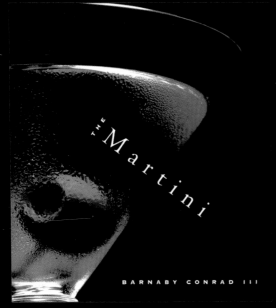

Typical examples by well-meaning colleagues.

years and see what those covers look like. They won't last." He might be right. But beyond spaced out type, the important thing is a confidence of your design sense. This is difficult. Current fashion shouldn't send you off like a hot dog wrapper in the wind. If you look at what you do today, it should look like something you would do tomorrow.

**—John Miller, Interactive Bureau**

The rules of not letterspacing lowercase and not setting type in all caps come from traditional typography, as does the rule of double-spacing small caps. These are how they used to do various craftsmanship projects, such as mortising the corners of the building. There was a very certain way of doing it. It wasn't as if you could do it like this or you could do it like that. NO! You did it like this. A lot of the rules are based on traditional typography and traditional design. That can be confused—or perhaps correctly associated—with being fuddy-duddies.

**—Theo Fells, Interactive Bureau**

# 6.

## Never set a lot of text type in all caps.

It's much harder to read.
(Exception: Hunter S. Thompson.)

Fonts were not intended to be set in all caps. They were intended to be upper- and lowercase and have serifs and descenders and ascenders so that they're easier to read.

You need to be an editor as much as a designer. Even though it might look hip to do something, the bottom line is, skip it if it's too hard to read. Readability is a number-one concern for all of us.

Your approach to design should be very much like the old masters' approach to painting. You learn how to paint classically, according to all of the rules, and then

**Rule No. 6: Only Hunter Thompson can break it and get away with it.**

if you want to go off and paint like Jackson Pollock, fine. But you learn to do it the old-master way first. The new school says you don't have to learn the old way; you're not going to paint that way anyway, so why bother? Give up on all that. As a matter of fact, the new school says, you're at a disadvantage doing all that old stuff. You might as well just do it free-form, whatever you want to do, and then you will invent some new language. Just like David Carson. I guess it's up to the viewer to decide who is more successful.

—**John Schmitz, Interactive Bureau**

# 7.

### A cover should be a poster.

A single image of a human being—preferably Madonna—will sell more magazines than multiple images or all type. The same with books, ads, and home pages—the idea is to avoid the pitfalls of fads. Don't get carried away by the stuff that you see swirling around you. Design often loses its power when you fall prey to whatever is popular now, whatever the latest fad is.

—**Tom Morgan, Interactive Bureau**

# 8.

### Use only one or two typefaces.

Because of the total accessibility of fonts, we see designers employing scores of fonts on every screen and page. But designs are pulled together with just one or two. The best combination of two: one light and one bold. (Hint: This works with colors, too.)

It's like Italian vs. American: Italian design has intense laws, like what you can wear together. This color absolutely goes with this color, and you do not change that, whereas Americans wear whatever colors they want and go out with idiot sweat pants in all sorts of horrible colors and logos on them. American design is like a free-for-all. Disagree with that and you're old school, not up with the times.

—**John Schmitz, Interactive Bureau**

**The cover as poster: Rhonda Rubenstein's classic "White People" design for Esquire.**

Esquire

THE MAGAZINE FOR MEN

FEBRUARY 1992

# WHITE PEOPLE

THE TROUBLE WITH AMERICA

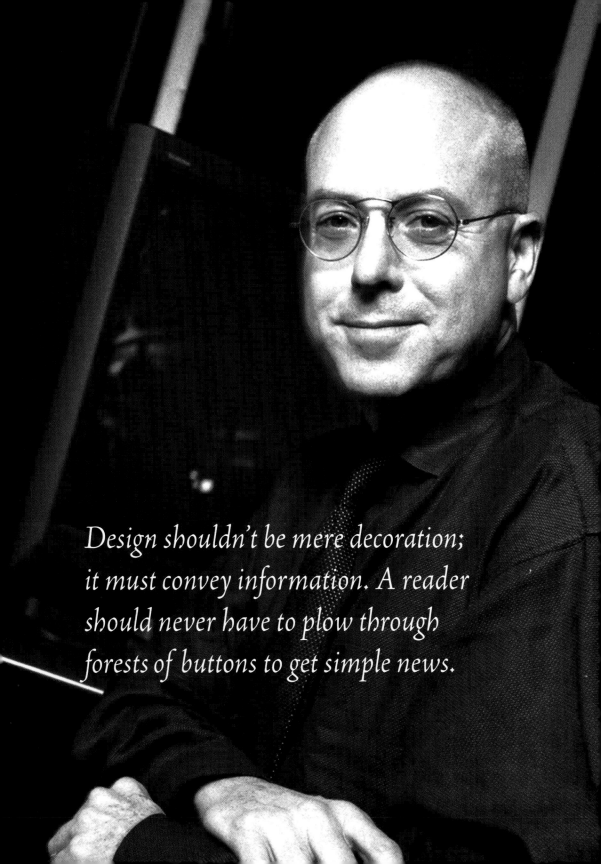

*Design shouldn't be mere decoration; it must convey information. A reader should never have to plow through forests of buttons to get simple news.*

¶ THE QUICK
BROWN FOX
JUMPS OVER
A LAZY DOG
———
pack my box
with five dozen
liquor jugs &
1234567890

# 9.

## Make everything as big as possible.

Type looks great in big point sizes. A bad picture always looks better bigger.

The Squibb home page is a good example of this. We scoured through all the vast resources of materials and came up with a couple of phrases that I thought defined the company to the public. We had been doing some sketches for them that were more scientific looking, using a molecule as a developmental tool. It was a 3-D look. It didn't knock my socks off. One of their higher-ups looked at it and he said, "Well, it's fine but what's special about it? What makes it *our* Web site?" I thought that was a really good question. I said, "Okay, what's special about Squibb?" We looked at all the other pharmaceutical companies on the Web. Some of them said, "We're the biotechnology leaders." Or, "We're the ones that do all the research." What I got from Squibb is they're the ones that are reaching out to you, the

The mission of Bristol-Myers Squibb is:

Rule No. 9: Interactive Bureau's big Squibb home page.

public: "We're the ones who care." So I said, "We'll put that on the front page." The chairman loved it.

**—Theo Fells, Interactive Bureau**

# 10.

## Get lumpy!

The trouble with most design is that it contains no surprise. Page after page of HTML type may be okay if you're running a scientific research site, but if you really want normal people to pay attention, you have to change pace.

What is lumpy? A magazine of consistent texture (say fifty-fifty text

Rule No. Pick a good-looking face, over 50 years old. You'd be safe with Goudy Modern (left), designed circa 1929.

# Big Picture

Two versions of our cover redesign for California magazine in 1986. Though the two images are the same size, the right cover's tight cropping and larger type make everything look bigger and give the cover more impact. Once again, bigger is better.

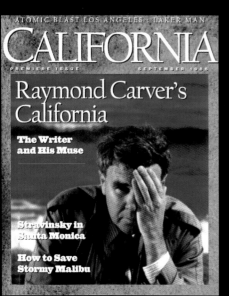

OKAY

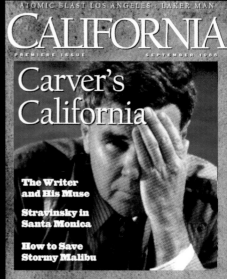

BETTER

# Big Screen

The Capital Group wanted a clean, approachable look for their American Funds site. We did several sketches: classic typography and vintage images on white backgrounds; a friendly feel featuring casual illustrations; and the more traditional, "financial" look. They responded partly to the classic type and partly to the friendly drawings. It all clicked when we combined the two and made the logo type much bigger. Now everything looked better and seemed more accessible.

**TOO SMALL AND RIGID**

**TOO SUBTLE**

**TOO PREDICTABLE**

and graphics) that suddenly runs three two-page spreads, or several pages with 100 items on each.

What we too often get is a monotonous rhythm of picture, headline, picture, text, ad, headline, picture, text, ad, and so forth. A pudding without raisins. A stew without lumps. Newspapers are the worst offenders. No wonder no one under thirty reads them! Why can't a newspaper occasionally run a full-page picture? Or a 10,000-word essay? Wake the reader up!

And why do 95 percent of Web sites have a graphic home page followed by legions of pages that look like mimeograph newsletters with snapshots stapled to them?

Look at the USA Today site. All those pages look consistent; there's never any question you're in USA Today. But it's not just picture-and-story. Some pages are all images, some text, some charts, and so on. They carry your interest from page to page.

The world is ready for lumpy Web sites.

It's more about having multiple points of navigation and entry, lots of stuff, lots of places to go. It's the same thing on a newspaper front: you want to have multiple entry points, high story count. Yet to avoid repetition you want to do it in a way which is sort of not easy to digest but which looks appealing enough to begin.
—**John Schmitz, Interactive Bureau**

*Web people don't care about your dumb design.*

—**John Schmitz**

# BLACK
## TIP

# Get Lumpy

**Lumpy design is best in newspapers.**

**Below: John Goecke's redesign of the**

**Baltimore Sun. A consistent look and**

**feel, with varied page layout.**

# What Not to Do
# on the Web

*An Online Primer*

# What Not to Do on the Web

**Rule No 5.**
**No Scrolling!**
75 percent of people
will only see this
much of your page.

Perhaps another
20 percent will stop at
this point.

Most of the rest
give up here.

Mad dogs and
Englishmen.

*Just as 75 percent of people will only read the top half of a folded newspaper, most browsers will never scroll.*

**J**ust as there are rules for good design—rules that work—so there are basic interface rules for things that don't work. There are some things, Roger Black thinks, that it is best not to do on the Web.

## 1.

### Don't repurpose.

If you have valid media, don't throw them out! The idea is to add value, to customize for the Web. When our office designed the USA Today site, we started with the flat graphics format the paper is famous for. Soon we realized that we could push this look further, that the Web version should be 3-D. So we took the paper's concepts and rede-signed them into wire frames that could be rotated, mapped with new textures, and eventually animated. The original content was still there, but now it was customized for the Web.

## 2.

### Don't confuse the viewer.

Your site needs to be consistently designed. If you have different pages and different sections, the navigational tools and graphics need to look the same throughout. Sadly, even in the most expensively designed pages, this is not always done. One is constantly tripping over new colors and new button styles. Sometimes you can't tell if you're still in the same site.

**Rule No. 1: Keep the good stuff.**
**(www.usatoday.com)**

## 3.

### Don't confuse the viewer, part 2.

If someone gets lost in your site, they'll never come back. Make sure your buttons and navigational directions are simple and clear. If buttons represent departments, don't add nondepartmental things to the button bar. And don't add links for the novelty of it. It's easy to get confused within a site; make sure yours is organized in a painfully clear, simple way.

## 4.

### Don't make oversize pages.

A common mistake among Web designers is forgetting that over 50 percent of computers have small, thirteen-inch monitors. Everything shrinks significantly from the artist's gaudy graphics monitors. Stop kidding yourself and design for 480-by-640-pixel monitors!

## 5.

### Don't design pages that require scrolling.

Just as 75 percent of people will only read the top half of a folded newspaper, most browsers will never scroll. People are much more likely to click a button and keep going. Shorter pages also break up the content in easy bite-size pieces, which is much more appealing to the viewer.

## 6.

### Don't use big, slow graphics.

To quote @Home's Richard Gingras, the only acceptable delay is no delay. Nobody wants to wait a minute for art or seven minutes for video—no matter how cool it is. If viewers have to wait, they'll leave your site and never come back.

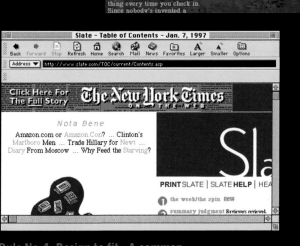

Rule No. 6: Don't use big, slow graphics. In our narrow-band world, there is no acceptable delay. (www.mtv.com)

Rule No.4: Design to fit. A common mistake among Web designers is forgetting that over 50 percent of computers have small, thirteen-inch monitors. (www.slate.com)

# Go Monochromatic

**Monochromatic pages look better and run faster. To avoid disappearing in all the clutter out there, keep colors to a minimum. The overall look will be pleasing to the eye, cleaner. The added bonus is that monochromatic pages load much faster.**

Simplified colors fly.
Top to bottom: Interactive Bureau's site (www.iab.com); their design of Font Bureau (www.fontbureau .com), and Genex's Porsche USA site (www.porsche-usa.com).

# 7.

## Don't use a lot of colors.

Monochromatic pages run much faster and look much better. The idea is to separate your site from all of the clutter out there. Web clutter is typified by freewheeling use of color, including omnipresent rainbow-hued buttons. If you get your design concept graphically right in black and white, you're on the right track. After that, if you want to, cautiously add one or two colors. Use red or yellow, but don't use them all!

# 8.

## Don't use blurry drop shadows.

If we never see another site with blurry drop shadows on every button and every speck of display type, it will be too soon.

Rule No. 8: Verboten.

# 9.

## Don't have a lot of text.

Nobody reads anything anymore. As we mentioned in the corollary to Rule No. 1 in the "Rules That Work" chapter, the only person you can count on to read every word of what you've written is your mother. Everybody else is too busy. Web browsers skim and surf. If you don't give them something quickly, they absorb nothing.

# 10.

## Don't use tiny type.

It's very hard to read text on computer screens. The general idea is to make everything bigger than you would in print. And make sure your type contrasts well with the background. If you really want somebody to notice something, make it easy to read.

# Classic Design

*Paying Attention to History*

# Classic Design

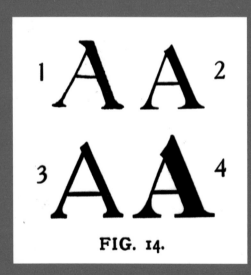

FIG. 14.

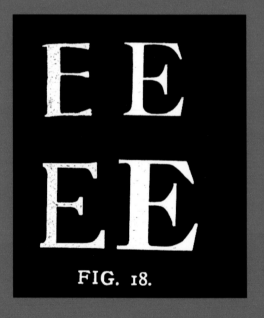

FIG. 18.

*A dwarf standing on the shoulders of a giant may see farther than a giant himself.*

**—Robert Burton**

**I**f the Internet has an age, it is adolescence. There is much talk here—chats, forums, threads—about the importance of freedom and comparisons between the Net's vanguard and our nation's founding fathers, "except," as Charles McGrath wrote in the *New York Times Sunday Magazine*, "these sessions, as often as not, are about freedom in the abstract rather than about the whisky tax or landlord-tenant relations. They're about the freedom to be free."

There is nothing adolescence hates more than experience or, more precisely, the voice of experience. To many netizens, Roger Black represents that voice. He comes from the dead world of print, they'll tell you. Those old rules, his rules, just do not apply here.

John Schmitz of the Interactive Bureau recalls a meeting he had with members of another design firm, young designers from one of the hot shops in San Francisco's Silicon Alley. Schmitz was showing them a site that the Interactive Bureau was working on. "They said it looked so much like print, and I said, 'Well, what do you mean by that?' 'These headers are at the top of every page,' they offered as an example. I said, 'Well, that's just basic site design; when I have that navigation bar there, that means that wherever I am in the site I can always go anywhere else. That's just navigation. Granted, maybe some people doing a site don't want that. Maybe they want it more free-form, more cosmic. But a lot of our clients want a fairly easy, conventional approach to navigation.'

"This was something that hadn't even occurred to them—to create navigational structure. The way they looked at site design was that every page should be really cool. It doesn't matter whether they relate to each other, or whether you know you're still in the same site; as a matter of fact, the way these sites are created is with thirty people in the room, and they're all paid four dollars an hour, and each one of them takes a page and that's called a Web site."

Yes, even in the world of the Net, there may be something to learn from history.

"There is a deep current of design that runs through the great civilizations of the last several thousand years," says Black. "You see it in the Phoenicians, the Greeks, the Romans. There is a small hiccup (though smaller than we used to think) during the Dark Ages. But it picks up again

quickly, flowing through the Renaissance and the classical revivals of the eighteenth, nineteenth, and twentieth centuries. All of this time it has been moving in one direction, carefully building on previous efforts.

The current of great design: Second-century Greek Antinous; Byzantine saints; Da Vinci self-portrait.

# Rolling Stone

# Patti Smith

### CATCHES FIRE
### BY CHARLES M. YOUNG

## Neil Young's
### WORLD TOUR
### BY PAUL NELSON

## Minnesota Fats
### BY ROBERT SABBAG

## Olivia Newton-John
### BY BEN FONG-TORRES

# THE
# ODYSSEY

### ...EARCH FOR LIFE ON MARS  *By Timothy Ferris*

# AND THE
# ECSTASY

"And all of this time there have been those who try to peel it back. Revolution is an old idea; it suggests by its nature the idea of getting back to roots, essentials.

"Emotionally, Modernism was an attempt to get away from the eclecticism of the Victorian era and the Beaux Arts and find a true voice for the machine age," Black continues. "But today we see Modernism as its own period. Significant, but not really a new direction for design.

"Another movement, from the same time as Modernism, was the Arts and Crafts movement of Will Ransom, William Morris, and the *Craftsman* magazine. Certainly, Arts and Crafts and Modernism were at odds—Ludwig Mies van der Rohe and Frank Lloyd Wright didn't waste too much time admiring each other's work. Yet today, Arts and Crafts seems closer to the human spirit of Western culture. Why? Because unlike Modernism, it was clearly building on the past; it was clearly a neoclassical revival."

**Arts and Crafts vs. Modernism: Frank Lloyd and Ludwig Mies van der Rohe.**

# The Craftsman

**J**ock Spivy and the Interactive Bureau are in the process of releasing a groundbreaking new CD-ROM: Gustav Stickley's The Craftsman. Adobe Acrobat Capture was used to do something that has never been done: while the CD presents exact replicas of every issue of the magazine—here's the kicker—each individual page is searchable.

"Gustav Stickley was the American successor to William Morris," says Jock Spivy. "From 1901 through 1916, he published 183 issues in all, comprising about 27,000 pages."

Using the Capture format, PDF Image Plus Text, Spivy, and an IAB team digitized every volume, creating a searchable, exact replica of The Craftsman. "There are complete sets of this magazine around," says Spivy, "but they tend to be in institutions and are hard to come by." Capture was developed to scan large quantities of documents—Social Security records, say, or insurance policies- while recognizing the words and retaining the shape of the page, allowing you to discard tons of paper. "What we've done here is to actually

# THE CRAFTSMAN

## AUGUST · 1903

**Vol. IV**  TWENTY FIVE CENTS A COPY  **No. V**

PUBLISHED MONTHLY
BY THE UNITED CRAFTS
AT SYRACUSE N.Y., U.S.A

- Stickley issues *Craftsman Furniture*, his final arts and crafts catalog.

**1915**
- Gustav Stickley, The Craftsman, Inc. enters bankruptcy.

**1916**
- Stickley attempts to retrench at 6 E. 39th Street, with retail space confined to the third and fourth floors.
- Leopold, Gustav and John George Stickley form Stickley Associated Cabinetmakers to manage the failed Craftsman Workshops furniture factory. Leopold assumes management responsibilities.
- The last issue of *The Craftsman* is published in December.

GUSTAV STICKLEY, A FEW MONTHS BEFORE HIS DEATH. COURTESY OF DAVID M. CATHERS

[ 70 ]

# THE CRAFTSMAN
## ON CD-ROM

A Demonstration
© Interactive Bureau, LLC, 1996

**Excerpts from The Craftsman on CD.**

[ *Gustav Stickley and the Rise of the Popular Press* ]

nearby."⁹ The twelve stories of Stickley's building were to serve as a full-service educational and shopping emporium for home owners and makers, builders, and artisans. Customers could even dine on wholesome food in complete Craftsman ambience at its top floor restaurant.

Stickley had finally realized his vision. But his timing was bad. Unfortunately the public had begun to move away from his ideals. Also, styles had changed and the country was in the midst of a Colonial Revival craze. Within three years, the whole Utopian enterprise was bankrupt.

[ 66 ]

## Table of Contents

use the tool for new purposes," says Spivy, "including aesthetic purposes. We've been able to create, in this digital format, pages which maintain the qualities of the original."

The Interactive Bureau is also hoping to archive The Nation, which has been published every week since 1865, in digital form. "It's an enormous undertaking," says Spivy, but one that suits the company's background in "old media." "I particularly like," adds Spivy, "the idea of being able to use new technology like Adobe Capture to make this material available to people who otherwise wouldn't be able to see it. In a way, we're not ever very far from print."

Gustav Stickley

CLASSIC DESIGN

**N**onetheless, the Modern movement has found recent exponents in print, notably Neville Brody and David Carson. No doubt Herbert Bayer and the Bauhaus would be befuddled by this Cuisinart style of the 1980s, ground up elements of Dadaism, Futurism, and Cubism—with a dash of a pure design grid.

"In some respects, Brody and Carson found themselves rejecting the cluttered eclecticism of 1970s print design," Black says. "Their work was bolder, stronger, cruder, and more exciting. Ultimately it inspired a giant horde of commercial imitators which, in time, strangled them mercilessly. In working for corporate clients like Nike and Pepsi, David Carson simplified his work—thereby co-opting his own style. It's inescapable.

"This is the problem with revolutionary design: it's like a flare heading to the sun. No matter how much energy you put into it, it just can't get very bright. By trying to break sharply from the mainstream, you have no true destination; you're likely more revolutionary than reactionary. It can be an entertaining interlude, but is historically pointless.

"Meanwhile, there is something to be said for building on the past, for avoiding novelty for novelty's sake. All design is suggestion. You try to evoke. There is a reason a book looks like a book. You could make it different every time, but these forms become pleasing to people or even whole cultures of people, so why ignore them? Familiar associations should be used to make design more effective."

Neville Brody panics.

THE resemblance BeTWEEN YOU AND andRe IS UNCaNNY BecaUse YOU BOTH aRe WEARING THE NeW AIR ChallEnge FUTURe tennis sHOE FROM NIKE WITH THe EXOSKELETAL STRAPPING AND THe HUARACHE-FIT™INNERBOOT system WHICH MOLDS TO YOUR FEET AND YOU BOtH enJOY THe BeTTeR LATERAL MOTION BEcaUse OF THe NgiTUDiNaL FLeX LINES AND HeRRINGBONE OUTSOLE AND YOU SHaRE AN INCReDIBLE aMOUNT OF cushioning HaTS OFF TO THe NIKE-AIR® CUSHIONING IN THE HEEL AND FOREFOOT AND THERe ARE

 MYRIAD OtHER THINGS YOU HAVE IN COMMON LIKe THE FOOTFRAME™DeVICE AND THe MiDFOOT tension STRaP WITH RUGGED HOOK-AND-LOOP CLOsURe FOR INsTaNCe AND

LeT'S FacE IT IF IT WEREN'T FOR THE HAIR aND THe earring AND THe WIMBLeDON

CUP YOU GUYS COULD Be. LIKe. TWINS. TWINS.

Reactionary design: David Carson takes the Pepsi challenge. One of the ironies of "revolutionary" style is that it becomes so popular, it's no longer hip.

The 1970s design of *Rolling Stone* surprised people because it didn't always give everybody exactly what they expected. It had classic design and typography with the Oxford rules; it always had a sort of formality about it. People loved that familiarity, but at the same time, there was a tremendous tension between what was actually being written and how it was being presented. I always thought it was particularly smart to have the youth culture presented in a much more classic, sophisticated way than the grown-up magazines.

**—Jock Spivy, Interactive Bureau**

In the following years, designers Neville Brody (in *The Face*) and David Carson (in *Beach Culture* and then *RayGun*) changed the look of magazine design, violating traditional rules of design, turning graphic elements and a myriad of fonts on their ears—literally. The former professional surfer Carson, in particular, touted his role as naïf. "I entered this field as a second career," he said, "not knowing histories, names, and designers—my early work, a skateboard magazine, was described as looking like *The Face* and I was surprised by that."

**Thoroughly modern Brody.**

David Carson's design for On the Road.

Brody's The Face

Black calls Carson's work "unreadable." When asked about *Ray-Gun*, Milton Glaser said, "It is provocative and breaks new ground, but at the same time, the magazine doesn't seem to understand fundamental laws of communication."

Nevertheless, Carson's spirit, if not his style, can be felt all over the Web. Most sites tend to be simple; most of the people who build them wouldn't know how to complicate them. "The wild stuff is in the minority," says Schmitz, "but it's often what

Today, the home run has been sanctified in the language as an exultant synonym for success, along with knockout, bull's-eye, and bingo. But some people still take Henry Chadwick's line. They point out that in 1987 the Cardinals won the pennant and nearly the World Series with the fewest home runs in either league. They say, as Chadwick did, that base hits count for more in the long run.

But this is a delusion, and it's been eloquently refuted by baseball statistician Pete Palmer, whose sophisticated reckoning of "run values" (the formula now used by the game's bible, Total Baseball) reveals that between 1901 and 1977 the average homer contributed 1.14 runs, while triples brought in 1.09, doubles 0.78, singles 0.47, and walks .33. So sure, homers are showy.

But it seems they're worth the gamble. And anyhow, if it had been "Bobby Thomson's single," who'd remember it now, forty years later?

## For lo, the grass withreth

SUDDENLY, there some something new. An awesome machine, lurking in the corner, threatened to make it all happen in a great hurry. What, they thought, is this? This is some same text for Esquire magazine. It was a dark and stormy night, and low and behold there were still many

## The Sack Is Back

*uddenly, there some something new. An awesome machine, lurking in the corner, threatened to make it all happen in a great hurry. What, they thought, is this? This is some same text for Esquire magazine. It was a dark and stormy night, and low and behold there were still many pages to lay out. It was not yet clear who would do all the work, or who*

"One design element that has been very useful for me has been the dotted leader, or dotted rule (left). In the late 1960s, I used to pore over Peter Palazzo's fantastic design of the Herald Tribune. In the paper's Sunday magazine, New York, he employed a simple design tool—dashed leaders—to great effect. I desperately wanted to use these, but was too proud to simply steal them. I thought long and hard about this. Then I decided on an improvement: dotted leaders! I first used these at an LA newspaper. They're everywhere now, but in the early '70s, no one had really seen them just like that. People would regularly come up to me and ask, 'Am I supposed to sign on this dotted line?'"

**—Roger Black**

people point to when they talk about the cool site of the day. *Beach Culture* was once the cool magazine of the day. One of my favorite layouts there was a double-truck, solid black, with little tiny fourteen-point type that said, 'Surfing blind.' That was it. But not everybody can do that. It was more of an art project than an editorial project."

"The real problem for a designer today is to find some deep water," says Black, "lest they run aground. The new designer celebrity and the sophistication of the consumer makes this no easier. So where does one look? Certainly the 1990s have shown no clear design movements: in print and on the Web, you see multiple examples of revivalism of recent periods, but very little satisfying or original work.

"So the challenge remains. But if you spend some time acquiring history about design forms, you're way ahead. You'll gain a sense of where we've been—and maybe even where to go."

# Where Am I?

*The Importance of Navigation*

# Where Am I?

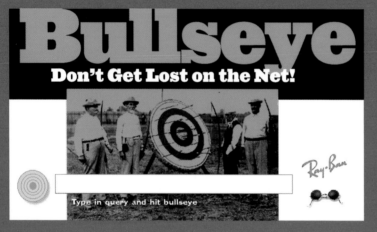

Don't get lost on the Net!
This early prototype for Excite
(originally called Bullseye)
shows Black's obsession with
clear navigation.

*What if you want to go from*
*the seventeenth floor to the forty-second?*

**W**hen you go to a Web site it's different than turning on the television and choosing the thirty-minute program or the sixty-minute documentary. It's different than picking up a book with 150 pages or 900 pages, or a newspaper with three or seven sections. People don't understand what they're approaching. What we constantly hear from people when they visit a Web site for the first time is, "I had a really hard time finding my way around."

**—Jock Spivy, Interactive Bureau**

Because of the layers in which Web sites are built, navigation's job might be likened to an elevator in a high-rise building. You start on the ground floor and work your way up to the penthouse, or vice versa.

But what if you want to go from the seventeenth floor to the forty-second? Or to the mezzanine from the roof? What if you want to leave that building entirely and jump to another skyscraper? How do you know when you've left the building, and having left, how do you get back? How do you know where you are?

"Don't assume that viewers will grasp the structure of your Web site," says Black. "You may design an intricate hierarchy, boasting a home page and various theme pages, subtheme pages, and so on. But once people have left the first page and begin frantically clicking around, they've lost all concept of your organization; all of the pages are completely equal. Your linear hierarchy is reduced to a horizontal mess in a matter of seconds.

"It's very important to always tell the viewer exactly where they are and how to get back."

All Web sites strive to keep their users coming back—from the cosmos that is the World Wide Web, and even within the site itself.

"You've got to keep satisfying users on each level," says Black. "The worst things are sites that have layer after layer of contents pages and navigational instructions. One important aspect of navigation is simplifying your site: boiling everything down to as few pages as possible—with content on each one. The next step is to organize these in as simple a way as you can imagine."

You should take site architecture seriously. In many ways, how you arrange your information is the most important part of site design. It's no good to have cool-looking pages that nobody can find. A while back, we worked on the architecture for the search engine Infoseek. It was complicated enough that they consulted with the information specialists at The Understanding Business—the Access and Smart Yellow Pages guys—to ensure the master plan of the site was clear and user-friendly. We actually spent the bulk of the design time on architecture and navigation issues.

**—John Miller, Interactive Bureau**

**You always know where you are: Web sites could learn a lot from the newspaper structure.**

"There are a few sites out there where it doesn't matter where you are," adds Black. "Take Cybermad.com and Grrl.com. They relish the chaos. They're extremely difficult to design, and they rely on an organic structure with numerous happy-ending cul-de-sacs. And along the way are surprises, which interface designers call 'Easter eggs.' In general, though, they simply aren't as effective at delivering information."

"Clearly structured sites hold your hand all the way through," according to Black. Shockingly simple, with consistent, clear navigation tools on every page. This seems obvious, but look at how many sites change the look and feel of the navigation throughout. The user is never sure that he hasn't been flung into some other site. Bad idea.

"The navigation bar should appear as a friendly helper to the user. It should always look the same—simple, functional, and most of all, consistent. No surprises.

"One secret to keeping the navigation simple for the user is to limit the use of hypertext. The overuse of hot links springing people off your site in various directions will result in at least mild befuddlement. It's used for the sake of novelty way too often. Only add hypertext or links if it makes sense.

"Perhaps the most neglected aspect of navigation is allowing people to get back to where they were. Sounds simple, no? But too often the viewer is reduced to wildly punching the browser 'back' button or referring to the URL menu, which is basically an unreadable list of gibberish. There's no easy way of leaving a trail of bread crumbs behind you; the 'go back' button is the hallmark of a badly designed site.

The button is going away from the computer. You won't see them on the Netscape chrome versions coming out. It will become more like Internet Explorer, with the rollover experience, a CD-ROM reaction. All the prototypes of Internet Ex-

# Navigate by Image

www.toyota.com, created by
Saatchi & Saatchi Pacific and
Novo Media Group.

The navigation bar should be friendly and helpful to the user. The best way to do this is to create your page navigation with Photoshop image files. Images are better than hypertext, which tends to be confusing—and dull. Nav bars are easily created in Photoshop as GIF files and mapped to take the user wherever he wants. (Also, when the viewer sees them once, they're cached and load immediately on subsequent pages.) Image files also happen to look much better and add a kick to the pages. A lot of bang for the buck.

Helpful, consistent navigation:
the original Interactive Bureau
design of www.discovery.com

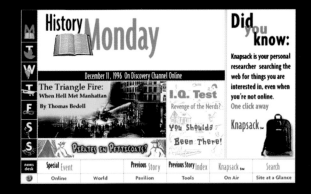

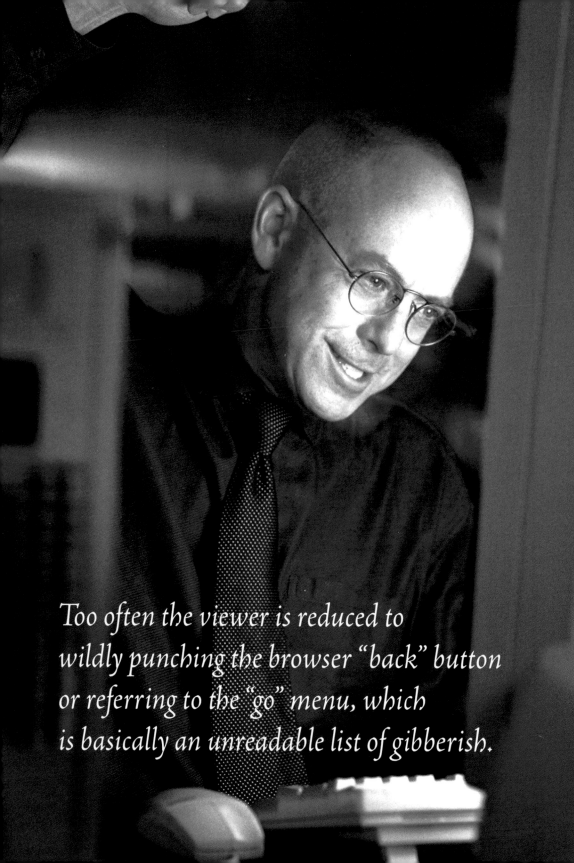

Too often the viewer is reduced to
wildly punching the browser "back" button
or referring to the "go" menu, which
is basically an unreadable list of gibberish.

plorer 4.0 and Netscape 4.0 are very different from what you're used to seeing now; they have a much more comfortable, consumer feel to them. The days of cold, hard computer buttons are going away.

**—John Goecke, @Home Network**

With new technology being developed every day, the temptation to complicate even the simplest of Web sites is great. It's the whiz-bang factor, the dancing salami that clients often want—and the first stage of building a good Web site is listening to your client.

I think the experience that designers have had with newspapers and magazines is astonishingly good training. Think, for instance, about what is in a newspaper. I can tell instantly if I am in the sports section or the classifieds or on the editorial page. It is something which obviously has been worked at over a long period of time in the newspaper business. Too many Web sites dump that content all over the floor. Navigation is what you need when you just want to find the funnies.

**—Jock Spivy, Interactive Bureau**

"I've spent years getting editors to rethink their content organization and presentation in magazines and newspapers," says Black. "This is a big part of a design or redesign. And, in certain ways, because people are less familiar with the Web, clarity of presentation is even more important here. And these all hinge on navigation.

"It really is hard to overestimate the need to simplify site navigation. It's safe to say that most of the time users don't know where they are. If a user gets lost on your site, he'll click the hell out and never come back. Run the risk of overexplaining. Make it painfully simple."

# Type

*Black and White and Read All Over*

# Type

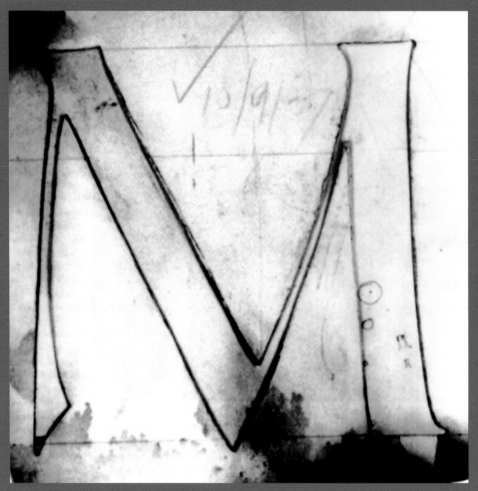

A Goudy pencil rubbing for Friar, dated 1937.

Frederic Goudy

**N**ow that you know where you are, you're going to want something to read.

Even given the Corollary to Rule No. 1, "Nobody reads anything," the truth is that the Internet is still closer to print than it is to broadcasting, and there is nothing more frustrating than meaningless or overused graphics. The solution lies in the right typeface, and here again the designer needs to take the classical approach—standing on the shoulders of giants.

The Modern movement of the early twentieth century seemed to be an abrupt left turn from the highway of traditional design. But even it attempted to get back to its roots. For example, the ultimate Modernist typeface, Futura, was actually based on classical proportions. Imagine the surprise of Modernist typographers when archaeologists in Crete unearthed fifth-century carvings of a typeface that looked a lot like Futura.

"It makes sense to dig into history to see what a certain font looked like when the artists first drew the face, as opposed to what happened when ITC got their hands on it. A lot of the type that we all inherited when we were doing desktop publishing in the '70s was a handful of the twenty-six typefaces that came from ITC, or type that was on all the basic typesetting systems.

**—John Schmitz, Interactive Bureau**

Along with Font Bureau president David Berlow, Black had made a name—and a style—for himself by resurrecting (or "reorchestrating" as Berlow says) fonts that were now "extinct"—which sometimes meant going back into old type books, stating the alphabets of these old fonts, and cutting them out and matching them with other fonts to set headlines and create striking front pages. It is that typographic sensibility—borrowing from the old to create something new which still has classical resonance—that has largely defined Roger Black's style, in print as well as online.

But with this new landscape come new rules as well. "It used to be there were a whole lot of typefaces that were made to be used very large," says Berlow, who, along with Black, de-signed type for *Esquire* and *Newsweek*. "They were very black and condensed, with little tiny white spaces in the middle—instead of the big white spaces you see in something like Helvetica. You couldn't use them below about eighteen points in print; online you can't use them below say 24, or 36 points. So there's been a shift in the possibilities, brought on by low resolution. That's the major thing that has changed, and it's purely a technical thing. Stylistically, you match type-faces to the subject matter the same way you did in print. You've lost all the capabilities of making decisions about text spaces like you could in print, be-cause they all work about equally well. So the faces you want to use online are the ones that have been made for online, if possible."

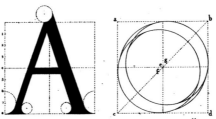

PROPORTIONS OF ROMAN CAPITALS. FROM DRAWINGS BY DÜRER

**Proportions of Roman capitals from a drawing by Dürer; Right: Smart Magazine's Belucian font, designed by David Berlow.**

# KEEP THE CHANGE

A FIRST LOOK AT

THE NEW NOVEL

# THOMAS McGUANE

SENATVSPOPVL
IMPCAESARIDIV
TRAIANOAVGG
MAXIMOTRIBPOT
ADDECLARANDVM
MONSETLOCVSTAN

Trajan's Column in Rome (second century), often cited as the model for Latin letterforms.

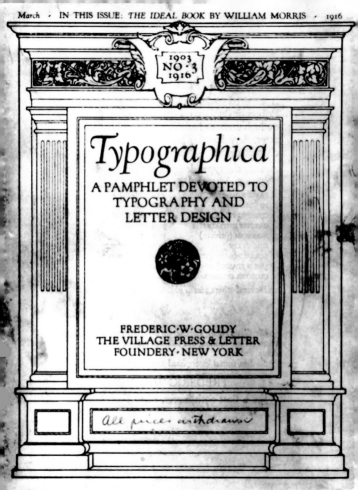

1903
NO · 3
1916

# Typographica

## A PAMPHLET DEVOTED TO TYPOGRAPHY AND LETTER DESIGN

FREDERIC · W · GOUDY
THE VILLAGE PRESS & LETTER
FOUNDERY · NEW YORK

*All prices withdrawn*

**B**erlow has been designing and producing typefaces for online use since 1989, when he did a lot of work on the Microsoft and Apple systems fonts. He had trained at Linotype in the 1970s, when Black was art directing *Rolling Stone*, and came looking for help in producing an original typeface for the magazine. By the late '80s Berlow was at Bitstream, the first digital typefoundry, and it was clear to him that "there was a need for more fonts than were available."

"Adobe had come up with 35 fonts when the LaserWriter was released, and by '87," Berlow remembers, "I think there were about a hundred fonts available. We wanted to have an independent source of fonts as desktop publishing moved forward, and I became disenchanted with the pace at Bitstream, so I quit in '89 and founded the Font Bureau with Roger. With a $15,000 credit from the leasing company! Operating out of my living room, we worked together to do a bunch of publications—*Smart* magazine; we did fonts for *Newsweek*, *Time*. We got a lot of

clients that had nothing to do with Roger eventually, and some he had worked with before we met, including the *New York Times*."

When it comes to describing the importance and meaning of type on the Web, Berlow likes to invoke driving down the highway—another experience not entirely conducive to reading.

"But there is typography on the highway," he says, "so at least for signs

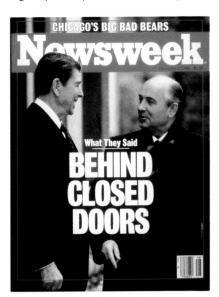

David Berlow and Roger Black developed fonts for a number of publications, including Time, Newsweek, and Smart Magazine.

# Font Frenzy

Just because you're designing on the Web doesn't mean everything has to look like computer type. Many font designers have come out with digitized versions of timeless classics. Adobe creates numerous fonts of legend, including Adobe Jenson used throughout this book. Black and David Berlow at Font Bureau design digitized classics, such as Frederic Goudy's Californian and Village.

Specimens ← → $ ?

## NEW HEIGHTS
### The Dark & Mysterious Amazon Basin
With a compass and a prayer, I went deep into the forest
## PALEOBOTANIST
UNSCRUPLED BY PESKY THINGS LIKE MONEY AND FOOD, I EXPLORED THE CITY
*Friendly tour guide thoughtfully dispensed with our valuables*
## CAMPSITES ARE NEARBY
*But don't forget the fondue pot: you know how it goes*
### Bachelor Pad of Humanities
A maelstrom of beer bottles and Chinese take-out food
## LATE-NIGHT QUEST FOR BEEF JERKY
## DIMES & QUARTERS

FB Californian
VIEW

In 1938 Goudy designed California Oldstyle & Italic, perhaps his most distinguished typeface, for private use of the University of California Press. In 1958 Lanston reissued it generally as Californian. Recently the roman was digitized for California by Carol Twombly; David Berlow redrew it when preparing italic & expert sets. Bold was drawn by Jane Patterson for the Font Bureau, who used it privately for four years before release.

David Berlow and Carol Twombly (now with Adobe) designed the digitized version of Goudy's classic Californian, originally created for the University of California in 1938.

Specimens ← → $ ?

## FRESH SPARKLING WATER
### METEOROLOGICAL DISTURBANCE BREAKS ALL RECORDS
## 35 inches of snow in only 2 hours
### ENTIRE TOWN CLOSED UNTIL FURTHER NOTICE
## STUDENTS WILD WITH GLEE
## Canadian Glaciers
### ENTREPRENEUR PLANS HOTEL & CASINO ON ICE MASS

Niagara
VIEW

While not a revival in the strictest sense of the word, Niagara recalls the crisp, elegant geometry found in some of the best American styles from the thirties and forties. The four condensed weights were designed by Tobias Frere-Jones, who found inspiration in the straight-sided geometric fonts from that era.

Niagara, a face based on 1930s and 1940s letterforms, was designed by the Font

| | HOME | UP | MAP | INDEX | SEARCH | PURC |
| Adobe | | | | | | |
| WHAT'S NEW | PRODUCTS | SOLUTIONS | STUDIO | | SUPPORT & SERVICES | ABOUT ADOB |
| WHAT'S NEW | SPECIAL OFFERS | PRODUCTS | BROWSER | | USING TYPE | TYPE DESIGN |

Browser    Families    Designers    Class    Packages    Previous    Up

## Adobe Jenson* Regular Display

Adobe Jenson*

# typograph

ABCDEFGHIJKLMNOPQRSTUVWX
YZabcdefghijklmnopqrstuvwxyz&0123456

ABCDEFGHIJKLMNOPQR
STUVWXYZabcdefghijklmnop
qrstuvwxyz&0123456789ÆÁÂ
ÄÀÅÃÇÉÊËÈÍÎÏÌÑŒÓÔÖ
ÒÕØÚÛÜÙÝÿæáâäàåãçéêëèfiflíí
ïìñœóôöòõøßúûüùÿ£¥ƒ$¢¤¯©'@
ᵃº†‡§₵*!¡?¿.,;:'"'"'"„,…‹›«»()[]{}|/\

| | HOME | UP | MAP | INDEX | SEARCH | PURCHASE |
| Adobe | | | | | | |
| WHAT'S NEW | PRODUCTS | SOLUTIONS | STUDIO | | SUPPORT & SERVICES | ABOUT ADOB |
| WHAT'S NEW | SPECIAL OFFERS | PRODUCTS | BROWSER | | USING TYPE | TYPE DESIGN |

Browser   Families   Designers   Class   Packages   Previous   Up

**Bulmer Italic Display**

Bulmer

# *typography*

*ABCDEFGHIJKLMNOPQRSTUVWXYZab
cdefghijklmnopqrstuvwxyz&0123456789ÆÁ*

*ABCDEFGHIJKLMNOPQRSTU
VWXYZabcdefghijklmnopqrstuvw
xyz&0123456789ÆÁÂÄÀÅÃÇÉ
ÊËÈÍÎÏÌÑŒÓÔÖÒÕØÚÛÜÙÝÿæ
áâäàåãçéêëèfiflíîïìñœóôöòõøßúûüùÿ
£¥ƒ$¢¤™©®@ᵃº†‡§¶*!¡?¿.,;:'"'"
„,…‹›«»()[]{}/|•¯˘˙˚¸˝˛ˆˇ¨ˉˋ´˜#
%‰=+~<>÷−¬^/.*

# Big Type

For headlines and large display type, Adobe Illustrator and Adobe Photoshop are the tools of choice. As Black explains: "Photoshop allows for very accurate letter-by-letter kerning. It's not ideal for large amounts of type, but when you need to get it exactly right, it's great." Photoshop also allows for easy customization of type: creating 3-D effects or introducing subtle patterns into type (select the letter and use the "paste-into" function). The trick is to push beyond those ever-present fuzzy drop shadows, which Black says are verboten: "I'd be very, very happy if I never saw another one."

Hand-kerned Californian Roman for the National Park Service.

In a pre-digital attempt at rationalism, Jaugeon,
a French scientist, projected every Roman capital
on a framework of 2,304 squares.

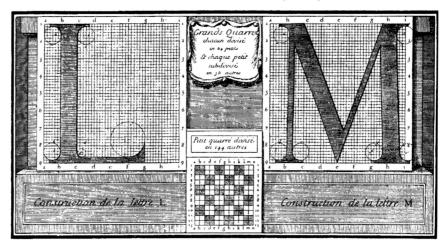

and captions and credits and buttons and all kinds of other things, there is still typography on the Web, and it's as important as ever." One single metaphor will not fit the World Wide Web, however (which is why you don't hear about the Infobahn anymore), and type on the Web serves a less rudimentary purpose than road signs do. "Type designers make typefaces for one purpose or another; there are billions of purposes. Online is one subset of that, and print is one subset of that, and entertainment is one. Some of them are working online— and some of them are falling apart."

Although the firm's library had been produced in Adobe's standard Type 1 format, Berlow became intrigued with the online possibilities of TrueType, a rival format developed by Apple Computer.

"Since Apple didn't adopt Display PostScript to drive its screens," he explains, "they wanted a way to use the same fonts on the screen and on the printer. Originally, PostScript fonts included a bitmap version that was clear on the screen. The outline fonts just could not be controlled to read well enough in small sizes, at low resolution."

"With hindsight, Apple developed a way to 'hint' the outlines, to make them produce a good bitmap in small sizes, and so we turned to True-Type to make scalable, printable fonts that work well on the screen," he says.

One early online customer for the Font Bureau was Prodigy, which hired the foundry to create typefaces for a never-released redesign, called P2, in 1994. Berlow chose Proforma, designed by Petr van Blokland, and Agenda, designed by Greg Thompson, and these were hinted to read well on the screen.

In 1996, Berlow adapted a new Roman type, Miller, designed by Matthew Carter, for @Home Network. Working with John Goecke, the @Home art director, and Black, they came up with a novel idea: to re-place the standard Roman bold on the Web, with a sans serif bold. HTML only allows for one "proportional" typeface. But by switching the bold fonts, @Home could give its customers a richer typographical experience. And since @Home service reps do the installations, they could set the preferences in the browser to their own custom font.

"Now Adobe, Apple, and Microsoft have agreed to merge the rival technologies into a new standard that will print as well as Type 1 and work on the screen as well as TrueType. OpenType, won't be easy, but it will be great to get everyone back on the same page," says Berlow. "Adobe is doing the work, so we can be assured that the big beneficiary will be readers, wherever they are."

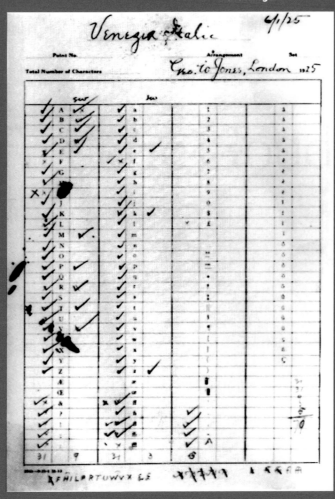

# Wheels on Fire

*Writing for the Web*

# Wheels on Fire

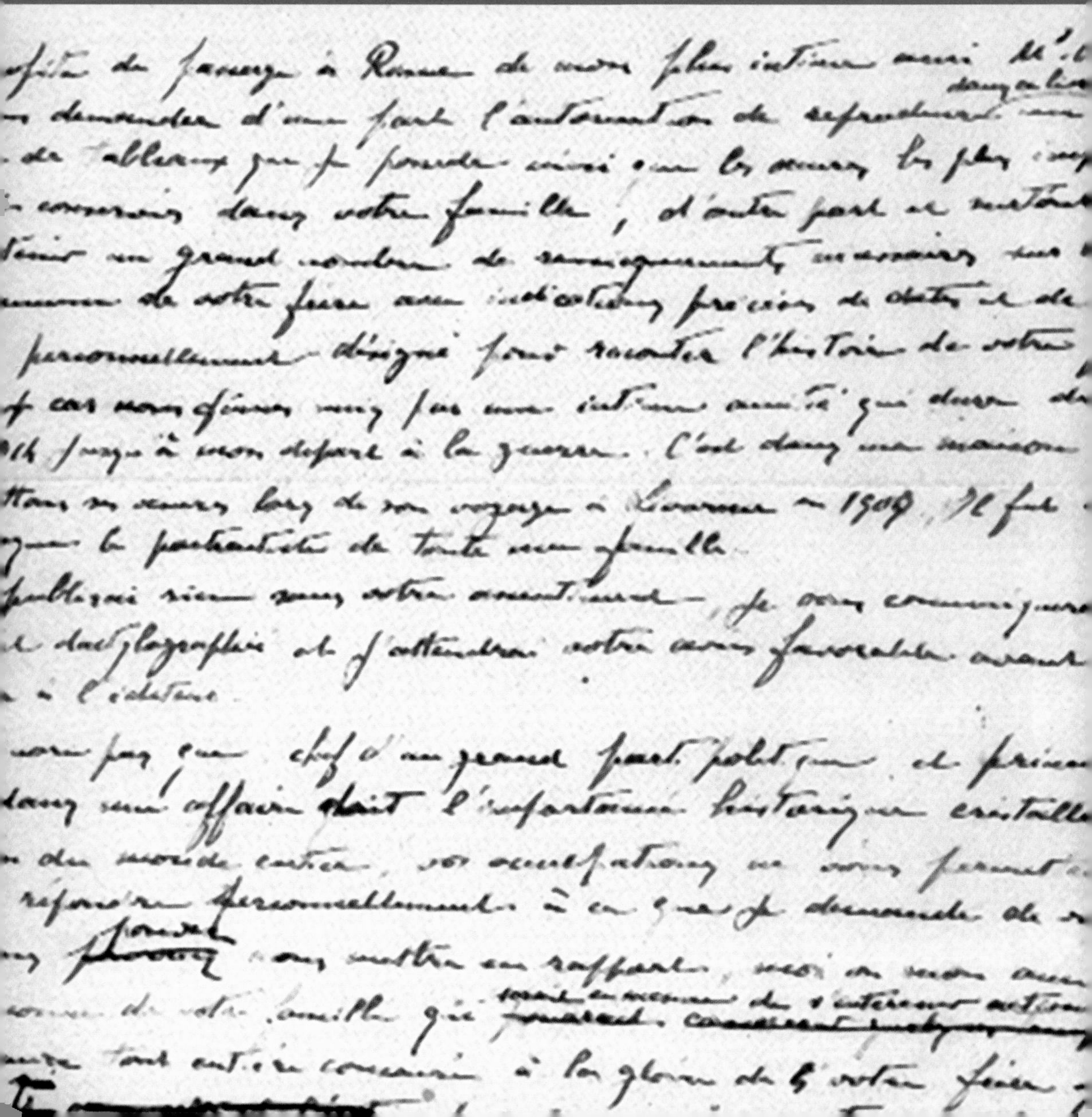

# New kinds of storytelling are what make a site really interactive.

—John Miller

One of the first things you'll hear from Web site writers and editors is that writing needs to be different online. They'll tell you that the old, linear print model doesn't work, that the reader is a user, a collaborator, and needs to be able to manipulate the information. They'll tell you that story structure needs to be broken and put back together, and if they are especially pretentious they'll quote Derrida or Roland Barthes and throw in one of Marshall McLuhan's fortune cookies for good measure. The whole approach to telling a story needs to be different.

The second thing you'll notice is how seldom it is.

"We have to learn new ways to tell stories on the Web," says Black. "The traditional, linear news story doesn't work. Take the Peruvian hostage situation [when the Japanese ambassador's residence in Lima was captured by a terrorist group in December 1996]. Rather than laying this out like a standard news feature about Americans and Japanese taken hostage, starting with who, what, where, when, etc., we should rethink the whole structure. Maybe the lead of this story is a strong graphic page with a provocative headline and quote that tells the story. For instance: 'The problem is that the Japanese always deal with terrorists, and Americans never do,' says a cabinet member.

"From here, the viewer can click several ways: to a map of the residence where the hostages are held, to an audio clip or video clip, or to a three-paragraph synopsis (only one screen scroll!), which, in turn, is linked to a more detailed story."

Traditional storytelling is linear. The inverted pyramid structure is taught to journalists for a reason: people want to understand the story immediately and then dig deeper— turn the page—if they want more.

But magazines use a number of elements to draw the reader in, believing (correctly) that a good lead is not enough. A feature story is studded with photos, pull quotes, and drop caps, all designed to draw the reader to the whole package. They are sideshows arrayed around the main event. The editor's job is then that of barker and ringmaster, and a well-edited story should direct your attention to all the surrounding elements while keeping your eyes on the prize.

But what if those elements were all part of the prize—if the tributar-

ies themselves formed the river? On the Web, a story can be approached from a number of directions; imagine the main story to be like the hub of a wheel and the other elements to be spokes. It should not matter where you begin, nor should it matter if you leap from spoke to spoke (via hyperlinks) and never reach the hub.

"Maybe clicking on one spoke takes you to a short story about who the Peruvian hostages are," says Black, "while another takes you to a profile of the terrorists. It's a very effective way of breaking up the story into easy-to-read, Web-size pieces." Ideally, readers will go away satisfied, without feeling that they've missed the main course.

**Work in progress: This Peruvian hostage crisis page is designed with a number of hot links leading to small, independent (yet related) stories.**

*Magazines use photos,
pull quotes, and drop caps
to draw the reader in.*

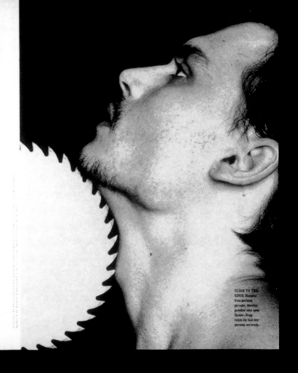

"Other than the obvious—avoid long, periodic sentences—I'd say that overall, writerly flourishes and rhetorical devices stick out like a sore thumb on the Web," says Marisa Bowe, producer of Word, a Web site magazine. "Long, winding, highly structured arguments are for print, not digital media. I think Web writing needs to be conversational and direct. I also think that if television is a cool medium, digital media are ice-cold, and the content needs to be emotionally hotter than it does in print in order to make up for that. I guess it's more like radio in that way—you want to read *voices*, not disembodied prose."

From its inception, Word (www.word.com) has tried to tell stories by using the medium in imaginative

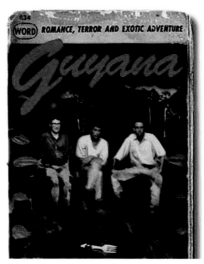

Word's feature on Guyana is accessed in various ways, including a link through a dime novel. (www.word.com/place/guyana)

ways—to allow the reader to manipulate the information without compromising the author's intent. In a feature Bowe produced for Word titled "Guyana," for example, frames are used to tell the story of three artists' journey to the rain forest. You can read their journals (filled with doubts, jokes, and gripes), look at appropriate images (sketches and photos of the indigenous flora and fauna), and listen to thematic music and jungle sounds—all while directing the experience yourself. An ISMAP in the form of an actual map of Guyana offers another way to approach the story, as does an illustration replicating a dime novel of yes-

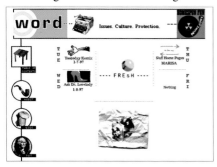

Word tries to tell stories in imaginative, Weblike ways. (www.word.com)

teryear ("Romance, terror and exotic adventures!"). All roads lead to Guyana here—and all roads are Guyana.

Consider the recent Picasso revival. Rather than slapping up an endlessly scrolling 2,500-word story about Picasso, break it up. The center, the axis, becomes a visually compelling page with links that take you to a feature about John Richardson, a virtual gallery of Picasso's paintings, a review of Anthony Hopkins' film portrayal, and maybe some saucy bits about Picasso's marriages. All these different spokes of the wheel—all of the pieces of the story—are written, edited, and designed to work on their own, completely independently, yet look and feel as if they belong to the whole. You can follow the specific path of the story that you're interested in. You don't have to make your way through wads of paragraphs to find something you like. More than cool buttons or fancy Java tricks, this is what makes a story interactive.

**—John Miller, Interactive Bureau**

Linking to other sites is something that many people with print and broadcast backgrounds are initially uncomfortable with. *Tell the viewer to touch that dial? Put down your magazine and pick up another?*

Exactly. Anyone who has had that first ah-ha experience online—who has really found themselves surfing—knows the feeling and how unlike reading or even channel surfing it is. It's as if you started in *Newsweek*, detoured to *Nature*, somehow went to *Spin*, made a pit stop at *Money*, checked in on some stylin' 'zine, and ended up reading a long piece in the *Atlantic Monthly*. Or each channel you flipped to on TV was showing something related to the last program you watched. As a Web site writer (or editor), you need to trust your audience to trust you, to remember your site as their point of embarkation, the place where their journey began.

In doing so, your site can become the hub in that wheel, and the story you are telling has the potential to become as large and surprising as the Net itself.

# Moving Pictures

*Video on the Web*

# Moving Pictures

**Listings** **Credits** ◀ **Jan. 11-12, 1997**

## CATCH SOME AIR

No **vertigo** is the motto. Fly, **spin**, crash and sport cool **gear**. Catch the **snow-board** spirit.

**Sports**

**NFL** Battling it out.

The vanguard of the Web's next wave: Internet access at lightning speed, here shown on @Home. It's the World Wide Web without the wait.

In September 1957, the peacock first revealed her color plumage.

*Wow! I've got color TV*
*RCA Victor color TV.*
*In our home there's color now*
*Wow! I've got color TV.*

**—RCA jingle, early '60s**

**W**hen color television was first introduced, most of the programming available was still in black and white. Color pioneers didn't have much to show for their purchase: Matt Dillon, Bilko, and Buddy and Sally stared back at them in shades of gray. *Wow.*

For people to want color sets, the networks had to convert to color programming (a shift that did not fully occur until 1966). Only when consumers became aware that something was missing—as the NBC peacock spread its black and white fan—did the sales of color sets soar. In order to sell the service, they had to create the content you couldn't get otherwise.

As consulting creative director of the @Home Network, Roger Black is aware of the Web's next wave: Internet access at lightning speed. The World Wide Web without the wait. Carried on enhanced television cable, @Home offers the Internet at a higher bandwidth, hundreds of times faster than a 28.8. A very fat pipe indeed.

But what good is that pipe with nothing to smoke? Most Web sites are designed for low bandwidth users. In designing the @Home Experience—the content the service offers as a gateway to the Web—Black and company have the luxury of making the site sing, employing not just Java and Shockwave but lots and lots of video.

It's very important to realize that people want to see video. They are used to it; they expect it. Television is the metaphor for the immediacy of the news.

**—John Goecke, @Home**

"In television, the viewer is locked in time," says Black. "There is an absolute running time for every show. Print is actually less linear than television, Marshall McLuhan's observations notwithstanding. With print, people can absorb content in whatever order they want.

"But the Web is multilayered. Text can be mixed with video, sound, everything! So here's your problem: getting people to absorb your linear text and sequences of video. The only precedent for this is CD-ROM design, which failed miserably: 25 percent of all CD-ROM titles produced sold fewer than ten copies.

"@Home is both a blessing and a nightmare. With broad-band, we're able to have video on every page. But we found that if we put in a fancy action adventure video that starts as soon as you open a page, it might be cool the first time, but when you come back to pick up another reference on the same page, you might not want to look at the same damn video again.

"Dealing with the video on your average Web site is a no-brainer: click and wait. Wait for it to download. Go on to another page, another site. Here comes your video. Now, why were you watching this again?

"On broad-band, everything happens at once. Lights, camera, action: an airboarder rolls down and out and back up again, in perpetual free fall, through the headline of an extreme-sports page. A real bull runs across

**Twenty-five percent of all CD-ROMs sold fewer than ten copies.**

**Black and @Home art director John Goecke.**

1. All type is created in Illustrator.

@Home Network has perfected a method of creating custom typography for its pages.

First, all type is set in Adobe Illustrator. Images and graphics are added and the page layout is completed in Illustrator. Then, using the drag-and-drop feature, the entire page is pulled from Illustrator directly into Adobe Photoshop. Here images are color corrected, and any final adjustments are made. The image is then saved as a GIF file and posted.

All of the original Illustrator files are kept, so future editorial changes can be made quickly and easily. Headlines are changed in the original Illustrator file, then dropped into Photoshop and resaved as GIFs.

2. Images and graphics added in Illustrator.

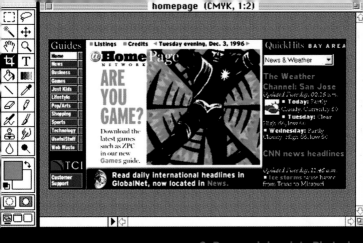

This allows @Home to use cus-

om typography and not be slowed

lown by changes in editorial.

Type that is brought into

'hotoshop is anti-aliased, unless it

**3. Drag-and-drop into Photoshop. Refine and save as GIF.**

# Self-Starters

With broad-band, everything happens at once: spinning GIFs, sound, even streaming video. The temptation is to use it all. But Black and his team became editors: every page was stripped down to give the viewer the sense of action without nausea. First, to assure the video would function cross-platform, they worked exclusively in QuickTime. Then they coded most videos to be engaged by clicking (each is labeled "video"). Not only did this ensure the audience would not be overwhelmed, it also solved the problem of browsers going back to the page and having to watch the same video over and over . . . and over again.

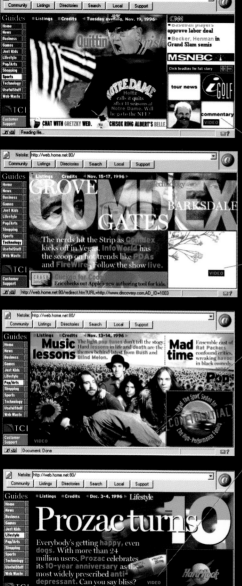

The top-level pages for @Home sections feature small buttons labeled "video" or "audio."

# Movie Effects

"We're always looking for new ways to get action and a sense of immediacy on the screen," explains Black. "The typical Web page looks like a mimeographed sheet with photos stapled to it." To this end, the Interactive Bureau has started employing Adobe After Effects. "It's great," says Robert Raines of the New York office. "It adds a lot of movement to the page. You can basically import Illustrator, Photoshop—even Quick Time movies—into one file, then composite them with the accuracy of

After Affects was employed to perk up this prototype for Infoseek. The map behind the top band moves slowly across the screen.

Photoshop: layers, alpha-channels, anti-aliasing, the whole works. It's also quick: you do all of your rough layout in a low-resolution version, then automatically revert to the hi-res originals for final display."

Dennis Rodman's chest. In the realm of politics, Clinton and Dole speak simultaneously, on the same issue, in separate video panels. The hard part is getting the words to keep up.

"We've gone out of our way to use bold, oversize Photoshop headlines throughout," Black says. "They get your attention.

"But there are certain hardwired facts about human visual response that you'd be a fool to ignore. Like if you put video on a page, a reader won't look at anything else. As animals we've evolved to be aware of any motion around us. It might eat us—or it might get us something to eat."

"What we finally settled on was a still from the video, clearly marked 'video,' for the user to click on," says Black of his motion-sickness dilemma. "Only in more visual sections, where users expect more spontaneous media with wildly spinning graphics, did we leave automatically loading video. This may seem simple, but is commonly overlooked even on the most expensively designed sites.

"The bottom line is this: if you have video on a page, let the video have the page. Nothing else stands a chance against it."

Today's Web may not stand a chance against video on broad-band. "When we send users out to a text site, there's a bit of a letdown," says Goecke, who worked with Black in print before coming online. "They are not going into a broad-band environment; they're going into what is set up for a dial-up environment. After being at @Home, the sites seem pretty flat."

Where some thought @Home might be but a door to the Web, the song-and-dance video environment is more like a lobby. A lobby where the stills move and the posters are better than the main attraction.

# Have It Your Way

*The Custom Web*

# Have It Your Way

Home page personaliztion: the new wave.

*When I go to a restaurant,*
*I want the chef to prepare my meal,*
*not the guy at the table next to me.*

—**Michael Kinsley**

**K**insley made that remark before the debut of Slate's much ballyhooed Microsoft Web site, and was probably not too surprised when hard-core netizens slammed him for doing what he set out to do: present a well-prepared meal. This was top-down publishing at its worst, came the cry from *Wired*. Kinsley, a former *New Republic* editor, was trying to colonize the Internet, they claimed, like Starkist's Charlie the Tuna, aping good taste when what the people really wanted was tuna that tastes good. Stale, a parody of the site, appeared immediately (www.stale.com).

"The whole publisher sensibility, where you would want to arrange your material in the best format for the reader, is something that enraged the digiterati crowd," says Black, who admired Slate, "because they take as gospel the idea that the customer, or 'user' as they say, would arrange the material as he or she saw fit."

What has attracted so many to the Internet and the interactive capabilities of the World Wide Web is just that implied freedom: to arrange things as you see fit. For years

Slate's editor-controlled presentation of material enraged digiterati. (www.slate.com)

now, netizens have trumpeted the age of personalization—the Web your way. Analogies have included the Sunday paper that is rearranged according to your specifications before it hits your door; the news program that opens with the weather or whatever you want to see most; and that elusive meal, prepared and served per your instructions—nuts to soup, if you desire, with a pause for palate-cleansing sorbet.

"I'm panting after personalization as much as anyone," says Black, "but there are problems. One is the response many users have: 'I'd love to do that, but I really don't have the time.' What people want is to kind of configure information around themselves without having to work at it. They don't want to fill out something that looks like a loan application.

It is no wonder that the sites that have succeeded in transaction—Virtual Vineyards, Amazon—mastered personalization first. How do you know what to sell your customers unless you know what they like to curl up with, be it Stephen King or Spinoza, and whether they prefer their Fume Blanc with a touch of oak or fruit? It is that bit of personal knowledge—even if it's achieved through robotics—that makes the sell seem less hard.

"The idea of building a customized customer profile would probably work better if some incentives could be added to make it fun," says Black. "What you need to do is figure out a way to say, 'You seem to like this, would you like some more?'

"If you accept the theory that the two-way communication of the In-

Amazon's wildly successful bookstore site began with simple personalization techniques. (www.amazon.com)

ternet is more like the telephone than television, it is inevitable that site design be tailored to individuals. The relationship between a viewer and the Internet can be very intimate. The interface should reflect that one-to-one intimacy.

"There is something extremely personal about e-mail, for instance. It's a wonderful form of communication. And chat is extremely popular: it is said that more than half of the time America Online customers spend on the service is in e-mail or chat rooms.

"Internet customers are not just readers or viewers. And if half of their time is spent communicating over the Net, it is inevitable that they will want to stay in an active mode and not go sit on the couch and simply consume."

So it is fair to say that users want to order the experience, as long as it's not too much work. And they would like a site to know their taste in some things, though certainly not in all. It's between those poles—the desire for personalization and the right to privacy, the wish to organize experience and the need to be entertained—that the future of the Internet lies. How do you satisfy such seemingly disparate directives? The answer is surprisingly human.

"In the 1950s, we thought robots would be mechanical humans," says Black. "Forty years later, we barely have robots bolting on car doors. We've learned they're only good for individual tasks and only in numbers can they imitate what humans do.

"The robotics part of personalization is agenting software such as Firefly (www.agentsinc.com.). This is a fairly simple application that builds a profile of customers' or users' preferences on a particular subject. For example, music. On Firefly, you rank albums, groups, and songs according to what you like. After you rank several lists, the software builds a profile of your taste and compares it to others. Then, like the old-fashioned clerk in a record store who knew your tastes, it recommends what you might like— that is, what is missing from your list that appears on the lists of those with similar profiles. Agents Inc. and its

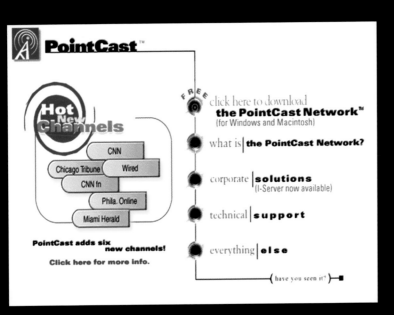

Pointcast screens dynamically conform to user preferences. (www.pointcast.com)

With Firefly, you rank music you know you like, and, suddenly, it tells you what you will like. (www.agentsinc.com)

competitors are rolling these and other "comparative filtering" programs out as fast as they can.

"But can these programs really be scaled? A thousand profiles work well, but when you increase to a million profiles, they start to gray out until they are uselessly general. A second problem is with the wild card in people's tastes. @Home's Michael Schwartz explains: a husband and wife may share the same tastes in literature, food, and interior design, but the husband may have a rabid penchant for Sylvester Stallone action movies. So the agent software may get tripped up and idiotically suggest to the wife that *Rocky III* is on TV tonight."

Just as the wild card problem could be solved with a little human supervision (or separate accounts, such as in the Stallone case), so the dangers inherent in personalized news—whose reductio ad absurdum would be a home page literally about your home—can be avoided with an old-fashioned editor.

Take Pointcast (www.pointcast. com), for instance, which allows users to select categories of news, enter the stocks they want to track, and so on, while the screen dynamically conforms to these preferences. "While this may be intriguing," says Black, "it only solves part of the problem. If you're normally not interested in weather, for instance, you may not be

*There needs to be a section added to these pages called "Randomly Interesting Stuff."*

alerted that there is a tornado heading your way. There needs to be a section added to these pages called 'Randomly Interesting Stuff.'

"This, of course, will need to be done by actual humans. But it is important. In fact, people tend to be most interested in things they didn't expect to learn about. (In the old days, we called *that* news.)"

Already there are a lot of very impressive, personalized features available, and a lot of services and Web sites. YPN (Your Personalized Net) is one we designed. You can really get a lot of things sort of surprisingly well-crafted. Even at this early stage of personalization that is available now—as agenting technology improves, there will surely be more. But one thing designers need to keep remembering is: "Don't forget the editor." The matter of the editor is, once again, crucial. Movies need great directors. Magazines and newspapers and publishing

houses need great editors. Online services and Web sites need great editors, too—and/or designers. It all goes together. But I don't think any automated system is ever going to be any substitute for a really fine, highly-skilled person making those critical, last-minute judgments— giving a site its tone, its point of view, and ultimately, its character.

**—Jock Spivy, Interactive Bureau**

"YPN (www.ypn.com) has an interesting version of a customized home page," says Black. "It allows you to select an enormous number of news sources and other bookmarks as it creates a personalized newsletter to keep you up-to-date on events as well as a surprisingly wide variety of Net content.

"While all of these are interesting directions, the question becomes, How far do you let users customize their site? Should it look like they want it to? Should they be able to pick the typeface, backgrounds, and design grid? Are designers right to override this, so that you're seeing everything the way they intended.

"Maybe it makes the most sense for site designers to create a variety of templates, so users could customize their look, but the site would maintain some brand distinction. For instance, you could have the choice of a Boomer site, Gen-X site, or Fogie site. Or maybe the Martha Stewart template, Nike template, or L.L. Bean template. Whatever the direction, it is time for designers to back off and give viewers more choice."

Choice is already the watchword on the Web. With over half a million sites out there, the Web is going the way of the magazine business, toward ever-greater specialization. (A few new magazine titles of 1996 included *Coffee Journal* and *Modern Ferret*.) "What we will want on the Web is *Single Parent News* magazine or *Boomer Single Parent News* magazine or *Brady Bunch Family News* magazine, much more than we're going to want *Time*," says Black. "But we'll still want edi-

tors—which gets back to how much interactivity people really want."

In designing pages for MSNBC, the Interactive Bureau had to keep in mind the preferences of users. It's important that they feel they are ordering the experience. "When people come onto the Web, they really want to feel like they're in charge and they're the editors," says John Miller, who helped on those MSNBC pages. "They want to feel like everything is at their disposal. So how do you let them continue to feel like that, but organize it and edit it in such a way that it's clear?"

As it exists now, says the Interactive Bureau's Theo Fells, who also worked on that job, "when you open

MSNBC's home page is highly personalizable—right down to your local weather report. (www.msnbc.com)

# The Personal Touch

The Interactive Bureau's design for Your Personal Net is highly customizable. Explains Black: "It allows the user to select from a number of news sources . . . and also creates a personalized newsletter which keeps you up-to-date on events and a wide variety of Net content." The personalization form is easy to fill out and is accessed right off the home page. (www.ypn.com)

The YPN home page and personalization form.

Fifty percent of the time America
Online customers spend on the
service is in e-mail or chat rooms like
"AOL Live" and "Mo Chat."

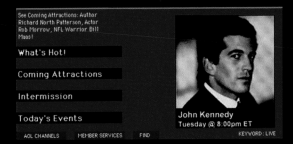

*For personalization to work,*
*you need real editors.* —**Theo Fells**

up that MSNBC page, you've personalized it. The news that you initially said you were interested in is
up front. But if there's something
crucial that day in the business
world, for example, there's still the
business section you can go to, and
then you have normal doors. Personalization, here, doesn't eliminate
the MSNBC point of view; it just
puts yours up front."

"Usually what you wind up watching on the news is the thing that is
fascinating to you that you would
never have selected," says Miller.

"Or if you look through a news
paper," says Morgan. "Maybe you're
following a story from page one to
the tenth page, and opposite that
there's something that you didn't
know was there, but you see the
headline and the picture. That can't
be done mechanically. At some point,
for personalization to really be effective, you need real editors."

# Transaction

*The Business of the Web*

# Transaction

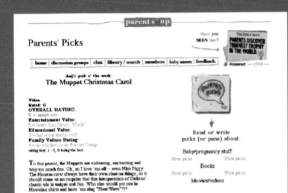

Parent Soup offers "Parents' Picks"—goods recommended by their users—for sale on their America Online site. (www.parentsoup. com)

First Virtual issues customers a virtual PIN which can be used at any First Virtual Seller's Web site. (http://www.fv. com)

*If you hook up a person to a product, you create the most welcome kind of marketing.*

—**Roger Black**

The first thing most people want to know about the Web is, What good is it? What's it for? You can have a better reading experience with a book or magazine (not to mention take them into the bath or onto the train), and audio and video are certainly better enjoyed on the stereo or television. Those who have staked their future on the Internet like to squint and envision a time when all those things will

Transactions are the natural business of the Internet, like flying is the natural business of a bird. It's not that birds can't walk—some birds can run, very fast. But what birds really do well is fly.

—**Jock Spivy, Interactive Bureau**

come together, along with personalization and direct communication. But in the meanwhile, visiting a Web site can be very underwhelming. You crash, you reboot—or maybe you go get a bowl of ice cream and see what's on the late show.

"If you think about it," says Black, "there are basically three activities on the Net:

1. Media, which is what most Web sites do;

2. Communications, such as chats and e-mail;

3. Transactions, which are really the primary form of business on the Internet.

"The Internet is not about branding, advertising, or promotion: that's

# Buying on Discovery

The **Discovery Channel Catalog** has mastered transaction on the Web. The wide-ranging site offers everything from the Power of Drums video set to just about anything you'd want about sharks. The site excels in a key area: matching customers to their merchandise quickly—without forcing them to wade through forests of screens.

done better in passive media such as television and print. Nor is the Internet about shopping—it's really about buying! Direct marketing works beautifully on the Internet when we connect a customer directly to a product and make a sale. Even airline, movie, and concert tickets—will not just be reserved, but actually purchased online."

The first step is personalization, discussed in the last chapter (see "Have It Your Way"). "If you can connect a personal profile to a product," says Black, "you create the most welcome kind of marketing. People are always more interested in getting direct mail if it's information they're interested in. If you're in the market for a car, the glossy Mercedes brochure looks a lot better."

Or take Virtual Vineyards and Amazon, two of the Web's more notable transaction successes. Virtual Vineyards (www.virtualvin.com) sells food and wine online by first building a personal account for each customer (credit card information is handled via a secure server) and then keeping customers abreast of vintages they've enjoyed before or foodstuffs (tamarind chutney, boysenberry-infused vinegar) their profile indicates they might be interested in. The tone is fanciful (the wine steward can be found under "Ask the Cork Dork"), and service paramount: most orders are filled immediately and delivered the next day.

Amazon Books (www.amazon.com) updates daily with features such as "Book of the Day" and popularity contests (cyber books are big), but it is touches like the personal notification service, which notifies customers of titles they've indicated an interest in, that set the site apart. (Parent Soup takes the idea one step further by offering "Parents' Picks"—goods recommended by their users—for sale on their AOL site.)

# Your Personal Net

Your Personal Net (www.ypn.com) was born in 1993, when Michael Wolff, a well-known New York magazine editor, was asking himself, What is this Internet thing? It was so confusing, and yet there was a lot of excitement about the Web. Was it hype? The more he looked into it and thought about it the more he understood.

"Everything is being digitized," he explains. "All media, all entertainment. The Internet is just the means of delivery for digital stuff. And if everything is going digital, then the

The web has become a battle for the home page, and the objective here was to make a page so indispensable that people would change the preferences in their browser to YPN.com. Steve Gullo and John Schmitz devised a solution (above) that tried to fill a number of requirements. Maybe too many. Gullo followed the work to Wolff New Media as creative director, and soon addressed the tension between trying to do everything and trying to make it simple (and fast-loading) for the user. The newest home page (left) is calmer, and there is quicker navigation to the reviews (perhaps the most complete and entertaining on the Web).

**Your Personal Net**

**gallery**
AT AN ONLINE SPACE NEAR YOU

**PICKS**
THE BEST OF WHAT'S ON

**netclock**
your personal
www.netclock.com

SONY-IMAX THEATRE
LS
FIRST CITY IN SPACE

Friday, January 31, 1997

**Electronic music at 9 pm ET on Pseudo Online**

**TODAY**
8:00 pm ET
on AudioNet
Tune into college basketball as Delaware and Drexel face off.

**TODAY**
10:00 pm ET
on AOL
Ed Begley Jr. of "St. Elsewhere" on his career and the environment.

**TOMORROW**
7:30 pm ET
on Irving Plaza
ABBA impersonators Bjorn Again play live in concert.

Your NetClock is set to Eastern Time until you join or sign in.

**CustomCLOCKSEARCH**

*Show* [ Entertainment ]  *for* [ Sat ]  [ 10 pm ]  *on* [ Internet ]

_____ *Start Search* ◉

**Today's ClickCLOCK**

PM 3 4 5 6 7 8 9 10 11 MIDNIGHT AM 1 2 3 4 5 6 7 8 9 10 11 NOON PM 1 2

**Browse the WEEK AHEAD**

| Today | Saturday | Sunday | Monday | Tuesday | Wednesday | Thursday | Friday |

**About NetClock** ◉ | **Punch NetClock** Let us know if we've missed anything

Copyright 1996, 1997 Wolff New Media LLC

As Net events proliferate, it is hard to keep up, and NetClock tracks them all—from online chat to content specials. It's searchable, and the results are displayed in a graphic grid.

---

```
⌨ <webmaster@ypn.com,1-3-97,Your Personal Newsletter>
📎 🔖 Your Personal Newsletter
=================================================
ARTS & LITERATURE
http://www.ypn.com/mm-bln/genobject/entertainment/arts

---------- Event of the Week ----------

\ Nate Penn and Lawrence LaRose
  Wednesday 1/8/97 11 pm - 12 am EST
  America Online live interview and discussion
  Keyword: @odeon

THE RULES is the latest "how to get a man" guide for
women. Now Nate Penn and Lawrence LaRose have written the
ultimate guide for men. In response to THE RULES, they've
created THE CODE: TIME-TESTED SECRETS FOR GETTING WHAT YOU
WANT FROM WOMEN WITHOUT MARRYING THEM.

-------------- Sites --------------

\ The Thing
  http://www.thing.net/thingnyc/

If your browser can handle it, this avant garde site is well
worth the trip. With rotating online exhibitions by cutting
edge contemporary artists and reviews of current and recent
shows, The Thing tackles the art scene admirably, albeit
with a solitary focus on New York City. A live chat room and
an impressively active bulletin board guarantee you'll find
an opinionated opponent if you're looking to weigh in on the
ever-raging culture wars.

=================================================

HUMOR
http://www.ypn.com/mm-bln/genobject/entertainment/humor
```

The P in YPN stands for Personal, and NetResponse built a number of features that make it possible to personalize the site. One of them, the ability to make your home page, attracted a number of users. But the most popular is a weekly newsletter that gives you a number of suggestions on new sites, or new content, in which you've indicated interest. The newsletter arrives as e-mail, and with ability in Netscape or Eudora mail to make the URLs hot, all the user has to do is click on the link. Despite the personal delivery, the value is in the reviews.

nternet is only going to get bigger nd bigger."

Wolff wanted to address the bewildering confusion of the Net in rint, the medium he had mastered, o he published Net Guide, which ultimately sold 200,000 copies. This as led to more than twenty more uides to the Internet, focussing on pecific areas, like Net Chat.

These were like TV Guide for the Net, but with attitude, perspective, nd good writing. Wolff quickly realzed that he had a solid base for a web ite that could become a widely-used esource.

At first, the material from the books was simply repurposed. As it grew, Wolff realized that the site had to have a life of its own. His partners at the computer magazine group, CMP, didn't agree entirely with him, and Wolff sold the name NetGuide to them and plowed the money into a new company, Wolff New Media. He brought in NetResponse to provide the engineering, and Interactive Bureau to provide the design.

Now you go directly to these department pages, which take you through all the sites (on the Web and on the online services) in each category. For a more personal commentary, click on a related column that brings some criticism to the Internet.

HOME PAGE | SITE REVIEWS | LIVE EVENTS | COVER STORY | BOOKSTORE

**Dazzling Web Picks** GIST

CONNECTING TV & THE INTERNET

Today in Entertainment

**net movies**

Complete Online Event Listings

net clock

Ever since the Lumiere Brothers and Thomas Edison first experimented with recording and replaying moving pictures, the movies have been one of the most important cultural forces in the world. Aside from altering the shape of human consciousness–no small task–films have given the world a new language, a new economy, new celebrities, and more. Get your cyberpopcorn and hunker down in front of Film.com, Follywood, and Prodigy's immense Movies BB. Talk about current releases on rec.arts.movies, current-films and classics on alt.movies.silent. Draw a bead on Pierce Brosnan's debut as Bond with James Bond 007. Try to strain The MovieBrain. And do the time warp, again, at alt.cult-movies.rocky-horror.

**Contents**

Across the Board (22)

Actors & Actresses (134)

Classic Films (16)

Directors (33)

Encyclopedias & Trivia (14)

Genre (39)

Movie Industry (74)

**net STYLE**

WHAT'S HIP? WHAT'S HOT? WHAT'S LINKED?

## Blah Blah Blah URL

IT'S JUST NOT ENOUGH to say you surf anymore. You have to surf selectively. You have to surf with style. As Web sites fight for positions in our bookmark menus, everyone's wearing their preferences on their sleeves. URL-dropping is in.

" Things were going so well, until I saw his bookmarks."

If you consider yourself rather smart–or wish others would–begin by bookmarking some of the intellectual scroll-fests that have popped up in recent months. Make

Home | Directory | FAQ | net clock

**net BOOKSTORE**

BUY the books you want, UPDATE the books you have

**FEATURED TITLE**

net spy

HOW YOU CAN

ACCESS THE FACTS AND COVER YOUR TRACKS

NetSpy

"Part John Le Carre, part Internet for Dummies, Net Spy promises to teach you how to find out anything you ever wanted to know about anything–or anybody–on the Internet."
—JON SWARTZ, San Francisco Chronicle

**Browse NetBooks**

| | |
|---|---|
| ▸ NetCollege | ▸ NetSci-Fi |
| ▸ NetDoctor | ▸ NetSpy |
| ▸ NetGames 2 | ▸ NetStudy |
| ▸ NetJobs | ▸ NetTravel |
| ▸ NetMarketing | ▸ NetVote |

"Thanks to Wolff and friends, the cyberswamp may just have become a little less murky."
—ENTERTAINMENT WEEKLY

Completing the circle, you can order books, like NetSpy, from YPN

The biggest inhibitor toward being successful with online transactional businesses is that you have to give the customer a fundamentally better reason to order the stuff this way. Many haven't given them a break on the price in relation to their own catalogs or their own stores. While they may or may not be giving them better service and they may or may not be making it easier to order, you have to line them all up in a row. Cheaper, faster, easier. Pick any two."

**—Jock Spivy, Interactive Bureau**

Even as imaginative sites attempt to offer more to online customers, to bring the dream of one-stop, see-me-click-me-buy-me shopping to fruition, there is another impediment to the success of business transactions on the Web: paranoia. The same people who freely give out their credit card numbers over the phone and fail to ask for the carbon copy of their charge slips at a shop worry about typing in their card numbers online, "where anyone could get it!" (A few well-publicized hacking incidents have been responsible for much of the alarm.)

First Virtual (www.fv.com) accepts credit card information over the phone rather than the Internet, and then issues customers a virtual PIN, which can be used at any First Virtual seller's Web site. What you have done by signing up is create a separate account for Web-based transactions, which are then billed to your credit card. "Your credit card number is stored offline," the site reassures you, "on secure computers not connected to the Internet." The Java-based site itself, designed by the Interactive Bureau, "connects the customer directly to the transaction," says Black, "without having to wade through forests of screens. And per-

*Transaction is natural to the Net, just like flying is to a bird.*　**—Jock Spivy**

Virtual Vineyards sells food online by building personal profiles and keeping individual customers abreast of foodstuffs they might be interested in. (http://www. virtualvin.com)

haps most impressive in the long run is the fact that the vendor's server with the credit card information is not connected to the Web.

The Font Bureau, a First Virtual merchant, charges you based on the number of fonts you download and the number of work stations they'll be installed in. And Discovery Channel Online (DCO) offers a catalog with everything from the *Power of Drums* video set to a U.S. Navy Seals diving watch. The original Discovery site and DCO were designed by the Interactive Bureau.

"If you look at the original design of Discovery, you wouldn't necessarily identify it as a Roger Black style of typography," says John Sanford, design director of DCO. "Except the catalog area, where there is much more of a feeling of a classic use of typography."

While some react with fear and loathing to the idea of an online bank (which is basically what First Virtual is, charging you a fee to hold your money while you shop online), others see it as an empowering tool— and guarantee healthy competition. "There will soon be dozens like it," Black predicts, and the user will benefit. "The fundamental thing about the Web—it's shocking how often Web developers forget this—is that the customer is in charge."

# Size Matters

*Working in Small Teams*

# Size Matters

# *Crapulous intermediaries...*
## —Igor Stravinsky

**V**isit any Web site that works—not the site itself, but the actual physical space where people do the work—and you'll notice something: there aren't many people there. Certainly not compared to a national magazine. And even at those larger sites that are the domain of some corporation (Time-Warner's *Pathfinder*, MSNBC, etc.), those extra bodies are usually not producers, designers, or programmers—content providers, as it were—but marketers, spinners, and bean-counters. This is no accident.

"My career up to 1987 was a linear advancement on every level," says Black. "More staff, bigger offices, publications with larger circulations. I truly thought that this growth curve—this surging wave—was the drift of Western civilization, and I was there, happily paddling, front and center."

"But in the late '80s, after moving out on my own, I worked on the start-up of *Smart* magazine. We only had eleven people and some Macs. The amazing thing is that we wound up putting out a better magazine with an art department of two than, say, *GQ* with an art department of fifteen. Why? Well, the answer lies in what Stravinsky called 'crapulous intermediaries.'

"When computer chips are smaller, the electrons have less distance to traverse and get there faster. The chip speeds up. It works better.

Smart's stripped-down approach made for a raw, gutsy, more crude magazine.

Smart's small staff made for a close working of editors and designers.

It's the same with humans; enormous staffs don't work. European publications have long understood this, and they work streamlined. What desktop gave us was the ability to cut out the intermediaries, so that the person who comes up with the idea actually does the page. This seems elementary, even obvious. But it's something we've long forgotten."

"At *Smart*," Black continues, "Everything was more direct, less filtered. The result was a magazine that was raw, rougher, more immediate, more crude—stripped down. And this is just the kind of design that works in the latter part of the twentieth century.

"Fortunately, the economy of the Web dictates that we follow this crude path. And that's just how it should be. The small team is perfect for the Net.

"A single person can't be expected to know enough about design, writing, video, and sound to create an

Bare-bones Smart, 1984.

effective site. Knowledge of the history and technical aspects of all the various media is critical. But a small team, while remaining bare bones enough to communicate, can also bring together enough disparate talents to knit together something larger, a whole, a new kind of media."

*Smart* was the John the Baptist of desktop publishing: it was the first consumer magazine produced entirely on the Macintosh. Apple bought 7,000 copies and gave them to their salespeople to help spread the word. *"See? We weren't kidding. You can actually do this and it looks good."* Black's involvement was not accidental; by the end of the 1980's he had done his time in Silicon Valley and was preaching the gospel of desktop, getting the unconverted publications to move to computers.

"Not that Roger's that old," notes Jock Spivy, who was instrumental in the launch of *Smart*. "But there is an unusual generational thing working here. I think that other really superb publication de-

# THIS SIDE UP

Andrew Watson
works with no net.

ANDREW WATSON is one of a new breed of aerialists expanding the definition of circus arts. Born in London, raised in the English countryside, Watson never intended to be an acrobat. First he tried art school, then farming, then lumbering. A decade ago, when he was twenty, he became a commercial buyer of technical equipment. But after three years, his cushy office job made him restless. "One day I saw an ad in a theatrical paper for a circus school," he recalls, "so I went to the audition and got accepted. I'd never had any gymnastics, but within five weeks I was touring in a small circus, fire-eating, juggling, tumbling. Then I fell in love with the trapeze. It's ironic that in my previous life I'd broken thirteen bones. Now I've performed more than five hundred times without a net and never come close to breaking anything!"

Watson spent two years with England's famous Gerry Cottle's Circus but didn't get off the island until his act won a bronze medal at an international festival in France. "In Britain I'd had no way of comparing our work with other aerial performances," he says. But the lyrical virtuosity of his act provoked immediate offers from several continental circuses, and he went on tour with Germany's Zirkus Roncalli. In 1987 he linked up with the Cirque du Soleil, whose travels brought him to Canada and America. Stressing classical circus skills, Cirque du Soleil eliminated animal acts and reasserted intimacy of scale over the pomposity of spectacle. It also added character and plot as well as an evocative, unified musical score and sophisticated lighting.

Watson has now left the Cirque du Soleil, but he still aims to integrate his aerial work with highly theatrical art forms. "I'd like to take the skills of contortion, acrobatics, trapeze, and balance into the realm of the expressive arts and distance them from always being thought of as just awe-inspiring stunts," he says. "I don't see why they can't be combined with music, opera, dance, and performance art."     —A.A.

The modern aerialist
as Harlequin.

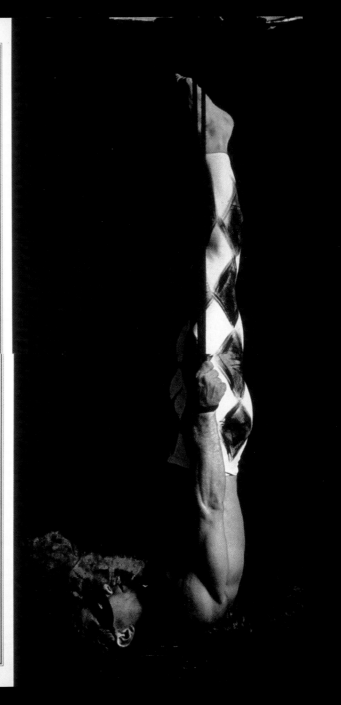

signers of his age or older have been anything but eager to embrace the new tools. Roger is quite unusual in that way. It has something to do with curiosity and wanting to do things as easily and quickly—and as well—as he can."

Even if it's preferable to create a site with a small team, is it possible? Yes, it turns out. Unlike publishing, Web sites don't have to rely on traditional distribution. So you don't have to run a global company to get your site out there. You can do it with a stripped-down staff.

In the magazine publications business, if you are not one of the biggest guys, you are at an astonishing disadvantage. Say you were armed with a billion dollars and wanted to start a women's fashion magazine because you thought there wasn't a good one. Say you wanted to sell it at the newsstand with a million copies in circulation. Well, you'd be thwarted. You simply can not get a top spot at the newsstand. They're not available. But the Web, by its nature, is a widely distributed network. It doesn't have a newsstand; there are no check outs through which everybody has to pass. Every time a computer is added to the network it's potentially an additional publisher and an additional customer.

**—Jock Spivy, Interactive Bureau**

# Tag Team

Working in small, closely knit teams creates less-filtered, more-immediate-feeling sites. The Parent Soup site is typical of how this works. The site was created by a team of three designers armed with the appropriate computers and software.

### THE PARENT SOUP TEAM

**DESIGN DIRECTOR**
Macintosh
Photoshop, Illustrator

**PAGE DESIGNER**
Macintosh
Photoshop, Illustrator

**HTML PRODUCTION**
Macintosh
Photoshop, PageMill

Finally, the thing that really allows small staffs to be effective is the advancements in tools.

You can have a small staff because the tools are good. Three of us put together the National Park Service site … with the help of Illustrator and Photoshop. These tools are powerful; they let you do the work of many. This allows for small teams, which makes for more focused sites.

**—John Schmitz, Interactive Bureau**

Besides being small, the teams that produce the most successful Web sites are generally diverse. Take Discovery Channel Online. The members of their production team—editors, designers, and programmers alike—hail from different disciplines. One came from a museum, one from radio, one from television, one from newspapers. Even the director of their digital lab, Omar Ahmad, has an alternate career in storytelling.

It's not remarkable that all these people can be found under one roof, working toward one common goal; it is, after all, a job. What's remarkable is that each knows something of what the other does, and they all get along.

Black explains it like this: "As one who has toiled all of his life in the vineyards of print, I've come to realize that I've lived in a hopelessly sheltered world. Publishing is an odd duck: it's a 500-year-old industry that is run like a medieval craft guild. In magazines, newspapers, and books, you see remnants of an antiquated apprentice system, where you learn —painstakingly—publishing's obscure methodologies.

"At the core of this odd system is a tremendous reliance on the creative process. All of us in the media take this for granted; it's simply how things are done. No editor has to talk a publisher into hiring writers. It is assumed that we know what we're doing and that we know what we need.

"In designing Web sites, I've been startled to realize that this is not the way most industries work. It is critical that people from print learn the way others work, starting with the concept of the product.

"The first time I heard a magazine called a product, I was appalled. (Mostly, I found it annoying that marketing lingo had wormed its way into publishing.) It's not right to call a magazine a product; it's malleable, its contents change. The same is true of newspapers and television. In fact, the reason people come back to these places is to get new content—new stuff. In every other industry, it's precisely the opposite: people keep coming back to get the same thing. This is why McDonald's worries so much about making its special sauce taste exactly the same in Topeka as it does in Bogota.

"In typical industries, the entire company is focused on product cycles. Product definition, in which all the features of this fabulous item are defined and related to market demand. Development time line, in which design and production are plotted. And the marketing plan, which spells out how the product will be sold and advertised and distributed. The process is the key to success, and employees are consumed by this methodology.

"In the media world, people don't pay as much attention to these cycles. I won't pretend that ad directors have no influence in publishing, but it's still the case that the most important piece of a magazine launch is the creative team. The same should be true with the Internet: if you bring the right people together and give them enough resources, and if they have the right ideas, you'll have a hit.

"In media, you deal with an unending stream of content punctuated by a whizzing series of deadlines. But this content—or news—dictates the process, not the other way around. Media loves nothing more than giant, overwhelming events which skew the deadlines and wreak havoc on newsrooms. This is the stuff of news! And it is precisely this chaos that every other industry desperately seeks to avoid.

"The bottom line is that the media is event-based, while all other industries are process-based. It's a very different way of thinking. Media is like American football; everything else is like soccer."

Being familiar with more than one discipline is key to making a site work. People that have experience in a number of fields are valuable. We don't need more designers who are only concerned with making pages pretty. Everybody needs to be as good an editor as they are a designer. Being aware of everything that goes into a site is extremely important.

**—John Schmitz, Interactive Bureau**

It is one thing for people from different media backgrounds to get along; at least their aims and assumptions are similar. Creative teams are by their nature more open to other experiences and outlooks—it is one of the hallmarks of creativity. But on the Internet there are other worlds colliding as well—the business and technological ends. The people making the freight must get along not just with each other but with the folks who are building the track.

"It will be much harder for computer businesses, telephone companies, home electronics companies, and cable multisystem operators to understand the way the media thinks than it will be for editors, directors, writers, and designers to understand the way the technology works," says Black. "And since the media are the minority in this endeavor, they are going to have to work much harder to inform the others if we ever hope to succeed in making the Internet something more than sophisticated software.

"So how do we resolve this clash of cultures? The first step is to understand our limits. None of us can do it all. (This is why AT&T, which is clearly masterful at their core business, recently abandoned all plans to develop Internet content. They realized they don't have the mind-set to make it happen: they'll leave it to others.) Once we

**Art director Robert Raines specializes in sound production for the web.**

## BLACK TIP

# Building a Site

In designing Web pages, the first step is sketches. Initially, several different directions are presented. For USA Today, these were done entirely in Adobe Photoshop. Even what would eventually be staight HTML text was dummied in Photoshop. Black and the Interactive Bureau use Photoshop files exclusively at the sketch stage. This is simply the quickest way to work and provides the best results. (It also makes pursuing numerous design directions much simpler.)

An original Photoshop sketch for the USA Today splash page.

Once a design is agreed upon, a prototype of the site is created. This typically consists of five to ten key pages, all linked and functioning. On these pages the type becomes "real." These pages are created using both Photoshop and Illustrator files, as well as HTML text. In USA Today's Sportsline (below), the top logo, Sportsline title, and navigation buttons were created as Photoshop files. Sections that needed to change constantly are in HTML text, for flash updating. Rather than run scads of dullish HTML text, however, Black chose to interspese custom type created in Illustrator, drag-and-dropped into Photoshop, and exported as GIF files. This method is ideal for sections that might change less often, but still need a custom look. Updating is relatively easy in this scenario. Changes can be made quickly in Illustrator and retranslated through Photoshop. When this prototype is complete, the remainder of the site pages are produced, all fitting within the design schemes of these key pages. The final product, then, is a seamless mixture of straight Photoshop files, Illustrator-created files, and HTML text.

DIAMOND RUN (left): June 94, Bonds hits a .75 and takes an end run for the finish to complete a sweep of the season. PASSING FOR DOLLARS (right): September 95, game 7: Bonds hits a .75 and loses his treasure June 94, Bonds hits a .75 and loses his treasure June 94.

Baseball | Basketball | Hockey | Football | Today's Games

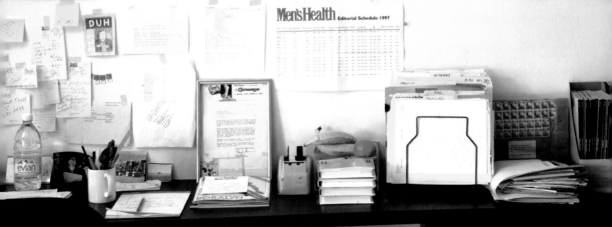

do this, we can ease the culture clash with common sense ideas."

# 1.

"Leave your assumptions at the door. We need to realize that our impressive track record in software, design, or editing doesn't mean beans here. It's time to throw away your Oscars, Emmys, and all the other meaningless awards. This is hard to do, as all creative people possess behemoth egos. But it won't work otherwise."

# 2.

"Build a team with representatives from each of the converging industries. And, if possible, hire people who have experience in more than one field. It is equally important to pull from different age groups and cultural backgrounds. These sorts of mixtures provide not only rich experience, but solid groundwork for cross-training."

# 3.

"Start cross-training. Get the software engineers to produce content, get the editors to try to write code. Get everybody to think about marketing. Your team members should spend some time in other areas, and hopefully begin to comprehend the scope of the project. Learn each other's assumptions, methodology, and vocabulary. Even basic words mean different things to different people: content means entertainment to a Hollywood director and data to a software programmer."

# 4.

"Set up a physical environment that allows a completely open process. Don't have the content department walled off from the marketers. It's important to continue to encourage any cross-industry communication that has been established.

"Part of this is physical. Nobody ever made a blockbuster working out of a cubicle. In fact, the old-fashioned newsroom had several virtues: the lack of claustrophobic work stations, and the open space where you didn't have to call someone on the phone to see if they were there.

Where paper still rules:
Roger Black's print design
Offices in New York.

165                    SIZE MATTERS

"Work hours are also important. By now we've seen an entire generation of burnt-out Webhead operations where underpaid college kids worked sixteen-hour days producing sites that soon crumbled, like them, from exhaustion. This approach, while still very common in the computer world, is shockingly short sighted."

# 5.

"Fund the content. In Hollywood, the preprint costs of making a picture are about half the total expenditure. In magazines, the costs before printing are about 60 percent. But in most Internet operations, it's a woeful 25 percent—or less! And don't think it doesn't show. After we're all over the flash of this new medium, content is what we have left. Spending up front may be painful, but it's the only way it will work in the long run. It takes money to build a new medium."

# 6.

"Keep your team from slinking back to what they're comfortable with. Recently, I was at @Home, casually eavesdropping on a conversation between a human resources guy and a software guy. Soon the discussion turned to the software issues of @Home, and all of the sudden the software engineer grew happier and happier. He announced that he was tremendously excited about what @Home was doing, then briskly walked off.

"I queried the human resources guy as to why our friend was so pleased. He replied, 'It's because it reminds him of home.'

"But we have to leave our comfortable 'homes' and stride bravely into this new frontier. We have to keep discovering new ways of working together. It won't be easy; we haven't even built this place yet. What we're doing is colonizing Mars—and we don't even have the damn oxygen in!"

Jock Spivy, New York offices.

# Client Tell

*What Is It That You Are Trying to Say?*

# Client Tell

*I'm not the dreamer of this film;*
*I'm the helper of the dreamer,*
*putting things in a certain way . . .*

—**Walter Murch**

**A**cademy-Award winning sound and film editor Walter Murch (the *Godfather* trilogy, *The English Patient*) once compared his job to that of a "dream helper." A dream helper is a therapist of sorts, but also a catalyst: it is their job to help the client (read: director) visualize the dream that is slipping away. "By the end of the session we have a fairly definite picture of what you dreamed, though when you came in all you could articulate in any detail was something about an ice cube. But I proposed these sometimes ridiculous options to you and they were the things you, responded to, defending your own dream.

"A certain amount of what goes on in the editing room is like that," said Murch. "I'm not the dreamer of this film; I'm the helper of the dreamer, putting things in a certain way."

For the Web site designer, the dreamer is the client; it is the bureau's job to listen to the client's dream and try to give it voice and vision. This comes from years of listening to people and learning to think like an editor, but it also comes from having a vision, of being confident enough in what you do and how you do it that your vision can accommodate someone else's ideas.

Interactive Bureau
Conference Room, New York.

CLIENT TELL

In redesigning magazines, it's important to go in and work with the publisher and editorial team to define the focus. This usually means entirely rethinking the editorial voice. Only after this is refined do you worry about how the pages look. It's the same with Web design. Initial client meetings are much more likely to be concerned with understanding what the site is about than with choosing typefaces.

**—John Miller, Interactive Bureau**

Black outlines his method of working with a client as a four-phase operation: the brief, trial pages, the prototype, and the launch. It's a model that would be helpful for any Web designer.

"A Web site that works is no fluke," says Black. "We've worked to develop a simple, straightforward, and highly effective process. It works."

First comes the brief, in which Black and members of his team meet with the client to listen to their concerns and offer possible solutions. "The first step in all this is to sit down with the client and have a big powwow," says Tom Morgan of the Interactive Bureau. "Really brainstorm. Really *listen*. If they have a site up, we hear what they have to say about it, how they describe it. Maybe they point to sites they like. Maybe they point to things they don't like. We can't do a very good job if we just go in and design a cookie-cutter site. Sure, we can make it pretty. But unless we really understand it, we can't make it coherent."

Coherence is key in a Web site that works. The design must complement the content and also facilitate for the user. The client has information, but there is a gulf between that information and a public they imagine is eager to find it, manipulate it, make use of it. The Web site is what will fill that gulf—and it can only do that if the client knows what they are trying to say and who they are trying to reach.

For the MSNBC site, Black created a number of very different looks for the trial pages. This strategy allows the client to react to a wide range of designs; it helps them feel part of the process. To the right are three of the dozen sketches originally presented. For this preliminary stage, each was designed entirely in Photoshop and posted as a large GIF file.

CLIENT TELL

# The Method

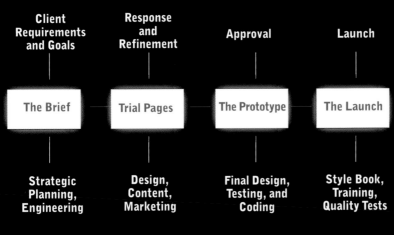

CLIENT

| Client Requirements and Goals | Response and Refinement | Approval | Launch |
|---|---|---|---|
| **The Brief** | **Trial Pages** | **The Prototype** | **The Launch** |
| Strategic Planning, Engineering | Design, Content, Marketing | Final Design, Testing, and Coding | Style Book, Training, Quality Tests |

INTERACTIVE BUREAU

## The Brief

The first step is the brief, a comprehensive description of the scope of the work. The brief describes what will be done by whom. It also describes the decision-making process.

All constituencies are involved, and a primary contact is established. As early as possible, a detailed site map is developed and any necessary media or software production is planned.

## Trial Pages

After the brief, the Interactive Bureau team creates a set of trial pages. These represent several approaches to the project, in two or three different styles. Trial pages contain enough actual programming to give the client a taste of the site functionality.

## The Prototype

Once a creative direction is determined, we move to the prototype stage. Here more templates and key pages are created, and advanced programming is implemented. Now the site has real interactivity and is placed on an actual server. Testing and optimization is built into this stage and continues to the next. Its successful implementation is key to making a web site that works.

## The Launch

Once the prototype is revised and approved, we launch. This involves the completion of pages and forms, as well as final programming. The Interactive Bureau frequently works with clients to hire and organize staff and can provide training, technical backup, and ongoing support.

When working with a large client, say Time Inc., you have to think about communicating with real people and communicating in a way in which the design structure becomes invisible. It shouldn't call attention to itself. On the Web, it's very hard to sell a client on that, because so many of them think that they're doing an advertisement. If *Time* magazine comes to you and says, "We need a redesign," they know what they are asking for. Even a magazine that is new might say, "We want a look that says *Fortune* meets *Rolling Stone*," but they still have some sense of their identity. But a large corporation like Price Waterhouse may want a site that's sort of wild. We did some sketches for their site, and they thought the design was too conventional, too old-fashioned. They had done an initial Web site, and their logo looked like it was for a skateboard magazine. We thought, *This is Price Waterhouse; who do you think your customers are?*

**—John Schmitz, Interactive Bureau**

The second phase is the production of trial pages: variations on the theme. MSNBC, for instance, was worried that Black's work on the Web was too much of a piece. They wanted to see something unlike what he was known for—design that did not look like Roger Black. While Black considers his work versatile, there's no doubt he's most known for his most original work, the core "classic" style clients keep coming back for.

"We just decided that we should try and throw as many different styles at them as we possibly could," recalls John Miller. "The division in San Francisco did a couple of hipster, not exactly classic things. And the New York office tried something sort of Neville Brody–esque, sort of new media–ish."

This stage is, by some reckoning, 90 percent of the job. "It would be easier for us to just come up with a single, strong idea," says Morgan, "but the client needs to be involved

*The wow factor isn't cool buttons or fonts.*

**Tom Morgan**

in the process. They need to feel like it's not just us imposing our value system on them, that we're giving them ideas and options. It's easier for them to pick one of three than for us to convince them that the one thing that we'd given them is the right thing, because they don't have anything else to compare it to.

In the third stage, the client is presented with a prototype, a final design that must be approved by the client before it is tested and coded. At this stage, the glitches from the trial process are excised and bad ideas that the client may have insisted upon are made to walk the plank.

"All key pages of the site are in place," explains Black. "You have a functioning prototype, with links and architecture in place. It's here we see how the site moves. This is where the client gets an accurate idea of how the site will behave on the Net. This is a very critical step, very different from looking at isolated page sketches."

*A great Web site is no fluke.*
*We've worked to develop a simple,*
*straightforward process. It works.*

GIC OBJECTIVES
Drive penetration in the consumer
market - early majority on up.
a singular focus on the
omer and take full advantage.
a strong, standalone
brand that earns customer
nded experience
mizable) and an
t can be
tent partners
Home
of emerging
compete
Windows
@Ball
Thane Music
PointCast
Sportsline
SPORTSZONE
Women's Wire
BULLS AND SIXERS CLASH
Raising the Titanic
Bil Gates video chat
CHANNELS
Kids' stuff
Bon voyage

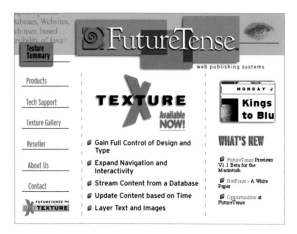

 infoseek

Interactive Bureau's online logos:
@Home Network; Future Tense;
Columbia University's 21st Century;
and the original Infoseek logo.

**T**he final stage is the launch of the site itself. Here the Interactive Bureau's technical assistance comes into play, but a good portion of this period is marked by good old-fashioned hand-holding. "It's very important to a lot of clients that they work with someone locally" says Miller of the San Francisco branch. "It's why we work from two coasts. Clients want somebody who they can call up in the morning and meet with in the afternoon. In this era of the Net and video conferencing, a lot of people really want the small-town, Mayberry designer down the street."

Clients are always concerned about finding that "wow" factor. They want people to really be blown away by their site. But the wow factor is not cool buttons or nice fonts. It's really the product, what the site's about. It's trying to express the original fiery vision of the founders or entrepreneurs, getting their message across, making it clear and accessible. The product or service itself should be the wow.

**—Tom Morgan, Interactive Bureau**

Black's studio has another advantage: its feet are firmly planted in new *and* old media. For Future Tense, for example, the Interactive Bureau not only built their Web site and helped with the interface (designing specific icons for the actual application), but also worked with them after the launch, designing their stationery and their logo. For Infoseek, Tom Morgan developed the original site and multipurpose logo. "For Infoseek, it had to look good on a thirteen-inch monitor and on the side of a bus! Two very different things," says Morgan. "It's important for designers to begin to think and develop on numerous platforms. It's really invaluable."

# Black to the Future

*The Net's Next Step*

# Black to the Future

VOL. LII. No. 6.    OCTOBER, 1896.    PRICE. 35 CENTS.

THE CENTURY
ILLUSTRATED
•MONTHLY•
MAGAZINE

**The Internet.**

**H**aving done umpteen hundred magazines and newspapers, Roger has a very strong, instinctive editorial vision, whether it be for print or online. He knows it's important for clients to figure out exactly what people want to use and consider relevant to their daily lives. Roger or his clients may not really represent Middle America. But he stresses having a good sense of what people find interesting, what their attention span is.

**—John Goecke, @Home**

When Roger Black tries to describe one thing, he inevitably refers to something else, which reminds him of a story, and soon he is off and running, the original point having been lost at the roadside.

This talent for analogy is appropriate in new media, the uncharted river into which all other media are but tributaries. Sometimes his metaphors are obvious (the telephone and television are the usual starting places when talking about the Internet and the World Wide Web), while sometimes they are quite personal and unexpected. But they are at least as good as anyone else's, as people grope toward a definition of the Internet's future, like the blind men attempting to describe the elephant. And like the blind men, the would-be seers can only describe what they know—their piece of the elephant.

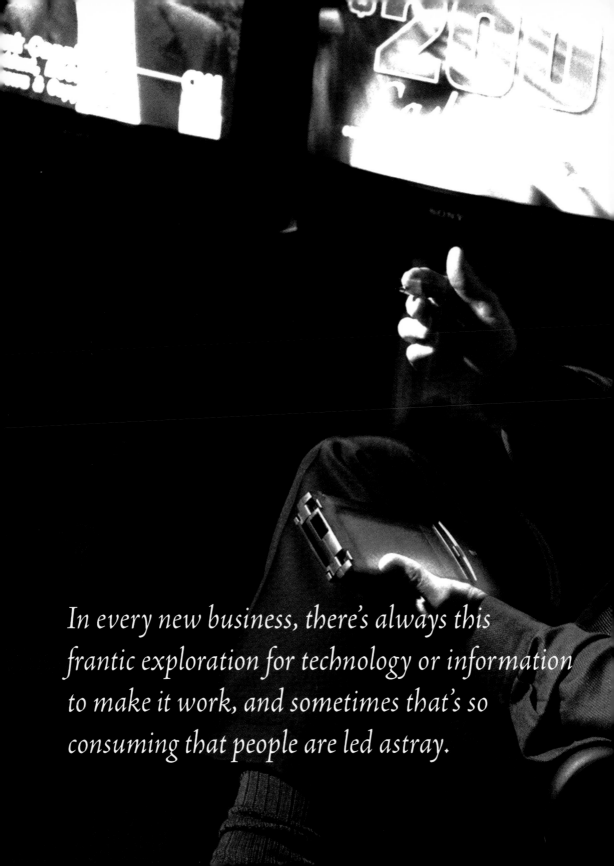

*In every new business, there's always this frantic exploration for technology or information to make it work, and sometimes that's so consuming that people are led astray.*

Designers should be familiar with the history of printing, the history of typography. It's something that has always informed Roger's work. A couple of years ago he went to the big French celebration they had for the Lumitype typesetting machine. He thought it was great; he said only the French would celebrate the anniversary of a long-dead machine.

**—Jock Spivy, Interactive Bureau**

"The phrase *new media* is really annoying," says Black. "There is no media integration in this medium. No one remembers silent films anymore—we know what they are in historical context, but they have no more meaning than looking at the *Century* magazine from 1895. That was the year that halftone engraving came into newspapers. They had the photographs, but they could not print them, so at the very end of the cycle, they would put photo emulsion on wood blocks and carve the picture out, carve the blacks out, and make a wood engraving and print that.

"It was very photographic in the sense of its realism. But as soon as photographs appeared in newspapers, they looked like something from another planet. From the very beginning of photography, people accepted it as reality. It's very odd. It was like, 'Yeah, that's it, a photograph never lies.'

"Print previously had been 95 percent type and an occasional cut. At the very end of the nineteenth century, they started illustrating it, when the halftone engraving was invented; then photography became integrated and was accepted very, very quickly. Not immediately. We're in that 'not immediately' period again now. But we don't even know what we're supposed to be accepting yet."

As creative director of the @Home Network, Black has become the lookout in Silicon Valley that the Interactive Bureau wanted. @Home is a cable modem service which hopes to bring the Internet to millions of homes with the speed—and broader bandwidth—cable offers. It benefits from the guidance of Kleiner Perkins' John Doerr, the technical wisdom of Internet guru Milo Medin, and some very deep pockets. This is a great place for a kid to play—lots of toys, no one pointing at the clock on the wall—and best of all, no one demanding Black define his role.

So it was that Mark Neumann of the @Home staff encountered Black while giving a tour of the service's headquarters to a potential partner.

"What are you responsible for?" the person asked Black.

"I'm not responsible for anything."

"No, no: what do you do?"

To which Neumann replied: "Roger does a lot of things, he's just not accountable for anything."

"You know," says Black, "after working for twenty-five years, it is very pleasant to get into a position where I'm not directly involved in any discussions about, say, employee benefits. Jock Spivy has been running the business side of the Interactive Bureau, while I've been free to absorb information out in Silicon Valley. And that allows me to go into Microsoft and say to them, forthrightly, 'You have to think very carefully about scaling. What happens if you go down the path of dynamically generated pages with this ASP technology that you are in love with is that you won't be able to hit the 20-million customer level. You will peak out way before that, and your servers will be choked up. You don't want to be in the position of Xerox in the 1980's, which became its own best customer.'"

The amazing thing is, Microsoft listens.

When I came on in November 1995, there was no proof of what the technology could do. Roger sketched out the service and what his vision was. Since then, we've gone through two or three managing editors and umpteen different trials and errors, and the service you see today is pretty much what he envisioned from the start."

**—John Goecke, @Home**

"Why does the new media exist?" Black asks. "Well, strictly speaking, it's a communications media. It's a way for people to communicate with each other, and that means in some respects it's telephone. Sometimes it's a multipicture medium and we are telling a story. There's some basic human needs that want to be fulfilled: we want to find out about other people. We want to find out about the rest of the world.

"In every new business, there's always this frantic exploration for technology or information to make it work, and sometimes that's so consuming that people are led astray. I'm from west Texas, so the obvious analogy for me is the oil business. People forget how hard it used to be to find the oil. It was buried underground, sometimes miles underground, out of reach of the drills. It was a pathetic experience, people wandering around west Texas, drilling holes in the ground but not finding the oil they knew was down there.

"Bit by bit technology came along that allowed them to test; eventually they could do what they called *wire-* line. Companies like Schlunberger made a lot of money hauling equipment around to set off little explosions: if it sounded a certain way, it would be oil; another kind of way, it would be rock.

"That situation is like our own today. We're just wandering around drilling holes in the ground, hoping that there might be something down there. And in the urgency to do that, in the kind of mad gold-rush feeling that's gone on in the last few years, we often forget that the things that

**Drilling holes in the ground.**

people want are the same. When the medium starts wandering off to some kind of abstract product definition that the marketing people dream up, it fails. Where intuitive thinking, writing, and creative work happen, it works—though not necessarily in the sense that the marketing people would like. Because it turns out that one person's intuitive inspiration may only appeal to two or three others, and not to the millions that had been hoped."

Movies need great directors. Magazines and newspapers need great editors. Publishing houses need great editors. And online services need great editors too—and designers. It all goes together. But I don't think any automated system is going to be a substitute for a highly skilled person making those critical judgments from the beginning, and making that first selection: thus providing tone, point of view, and character.

**—Jock Spivy, Interactive Bureau**

Roger Black:"In the early days of motion pictures, the director wasn't in charge, the producer was. This still varies. Some directors are producers some of the time, just as some actors are. If you go back far enough into publications, there was a kind of one-man band. Benjamin Franklin—he owned it, he wrote it, he printed it. And that was sort of the precursor to desktop publishing. But that broad specialization has sort of rendered impotent the designer or the editor at most publications. I think time will tell who gets to run these things in this Web medium.

"It's entirely possible that the designers will become the directors."

One-man band.

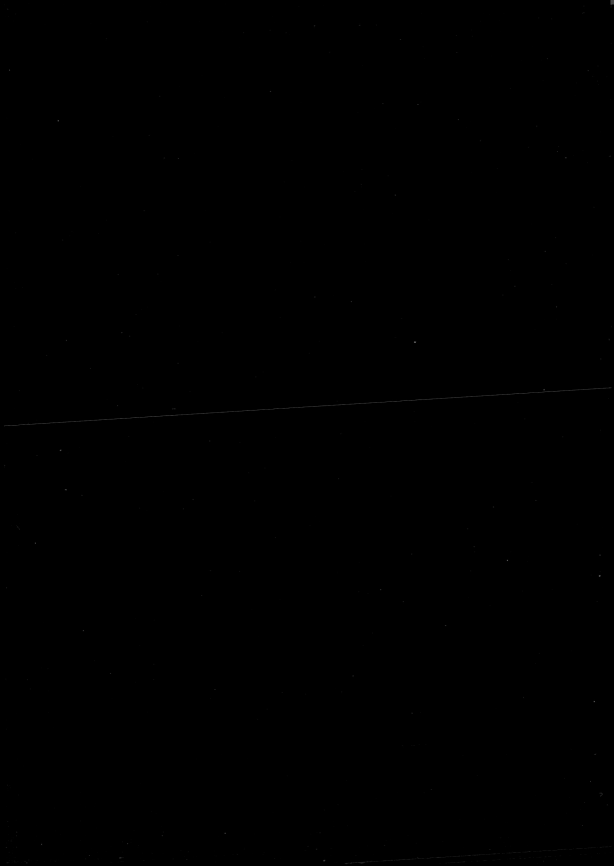

# Blacklash

*Roger Black and the Netizens*

# Blacklash

Black's design principles, including consistent use of classic fonts, are often a subject of controversy.

# MINERAL DEPOSITS

VE FIVE

# CLAIM

NE FIVE

# Stake in the Ground

VEN SEVEN

# CHARTING CANADA'S NORTHWEST TERRITORIES

E ONE

# GOLD MINE

VEN NINE

# A SMALL FORTUNE IN PRECIOUS METALS

VE SEVEN

# The vast riches of the earth are refined and sold

REE ONE

# FAMOUS CHEMIST

IE THREE

# Gives lecture at local University & describes theories

REE FIVE

# New Fermentation Process

REE THREE

# NEW SHIPMENT OF 82 PROOF WHISKEY HAS ARRIVED

**A**lmost no one approaching the World Wide Web for the first time has found a welcome mat waiting for them. Since it was introduced in the early '90s, the denizens of the Internet (or "netizens," as *Wired* founder Louis Rossetto dubbed them) claimed the Web as their domain. They, after all, envisioned the possibilities inherent in the medium first. They coaxed their computers through countless crashes just to look at the dingy, gray text-only sites that were the Web for years. And it is they who regard with great suspicion interlopers from other media—especially those whose names are synonymous with print.

From the day the *New York Times* ran a small item announcing the formation of the Interactive Bureau, Roger Black has found himself a ripe target for criticism. Reacting to the October 1994 *Times* notice, Neil Brainard wrote a scorching attack of Black in Hotwired.

"In his comments to the *Times*, the shameless Black managed simultaneously to acknowledge that 'we art directors have only a dim understanding of technology' and to announce the formation of a new firm that will advise clients on the design of interactive technology products."

It was not the last time Hotwired went after Black. In February 1995,

Brainard again accused the designer of charlatanism, pointing to a mock-up of the yet-to-be-launched Word home page (which Jessica Helfand and the Interactive Bureau designed and which Brainard deemed "a suspiciously Hotwired-like new electronic magazine") that appeared in Ad Age as something that "defies current HTML reality."

"I think Hotwired is one of the best things on the Web," Black told the *New York Observer.* "But they are suffering from an out-of-date, hacker-centric attitude about what is going on. I once said that appearing on the Internet without your own typeface is like going on TV naked, and they went after me for that. They attack anything linked to the establishment. It reminds me so much of the '60s it

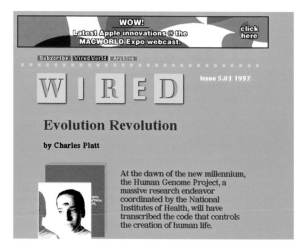

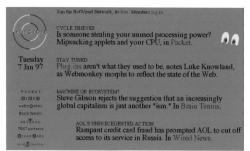

Wired's online version (above) and its cousin, Hotwired. (www.wired.com)

*I think Hotwired is one of the best things on the Web, but they suffer from an out-of-date, hacker-centric attitude.*

is frightening. Anything *Time* or *Newsweek* puts out is immediately suspect. They think I represent the old guard media establishment.

"You know, there was a brief moment when the techies had the Net to themselves, and they loved it," recalls Black. "So of course they were annoyed when the specialists arrived—the artists and marketers. But just wait until Eisner and Spielberg unleash their hounds—today's little rivalries will seem halcyon.

There's one of these newsstands across the street from our offices in New York—they sell everything: cigars, candy, and magazines from all over the world. I would go over there, page through *Wired*, take a look at the pictures and their drecky layout—in their very first issues, it was almost impossible to read. Yellow type, light orange background. And then I would go to their Web site and download it, and I made a little *Wired* format, what I thought *Wired* should look like. I'm exaggerating, but it was simply a book, one column, big type, and I'd just print out each article that I wanted to read in that format, and then I'd read it.

**—Roger Black**

It is hard to move from one interest to another without being labeled a dilettante. The very curiosity that has kept Black's name in play (moving, as he has, from print to desktop publishing to the Web) has caused some to accuse him of being mercenary—and sometimes even of stealing from himself. Just as critics sometimes said his magazines all looked alike, so Interactive Bureau clients have warned against being delivered a cookie-cutter design. Though as Black and his designers have learned, the cookie sometimes cuts both ways.

"Often people will come to us, and they will have seen something that we've done, and they will say, *We'd like something different*," says Tom Morgan of the Interactive Bureau's San Francisco office. "So we'll present a number of different ideas and they'll pick the one that looks like something we've done before."

"It is important for a designer to have confidence in their ideas. It's why people like Roger and Chip Kidd and Neville Brody develop

such strong, consistent styles," says the Bureau's John Miller. "If you examine Black's design of *LA* in 1972, it looks like something he would do today. That's the flip side of the cookie-cutter thing: he's been following the same ideas for thirty years. But it all looks great. Goudy, Brodovitch—a lot of people have spent their entire careers driving the same, reliable train."

What Black ultimately wants from the Web is what we all want: freedom. A freedom from the constraints of print and paper stock, from the realities of media that forbid type and video from inhabiting the same space, from the live nature of broadcast that controls time and hence the viewing experience. The control that interactivity offers is, ironically, freeing. And Black, like the rest of us (netizens or no), wants to shrug off those constraints. He wants to taste that freedom.

"I can remember in the early days, when I would work ridiculous hours at *Rolling Stone* and had to be up and do a thirty-six-hour run on dead-

Unwavering: Roger Black's design of LA, 1972.

# Who Owns the Beach?

Page 3

# LA

No. 5 August 5, 1972                    25¢

## GOODBYE MARILYN

abcdefgh
ijklmnopq
rstuvw
xyz

Canada to
seek max
for Keith
Richard

Memo

Memo

line," recalls Black. "And I would e-merge from the art department or the office and be totally struck that the world was three-dimensional. I'd walk outside, and the world had depth and shading and color. I'd been staring at all this flat, mono-chromatic world for too long. Everything was black and white. You would work entirely with photo-copies. Everything was flat, and the only dimension was caused by the layer of wax between the paper and the board. The two-dimensionality of print can be very frustrating.

"Almost everybody I know who's an art director has had other inter-ests; they at least entertained the no-tion of going into movies or playing in a band. I can't tell you how many design departments there are where you'll find a guitar against the wall.

"It's the reason that it's easy for me or other print art directors to make the switch to new media—it's getting us over our frustrations. It's like the art directors who do oil painting at night or on the weekends. Though I think it's probably healthier for you if you're a frustrated rock musician than to be a frustrated fine artist."

"Like it or not, the Web is much larger than any single discipline or even technology. It's multi-dimen-sionality will attract the best and brightest from all the professions, including the artist, the art director, and the designer. Like life itself, it's not about who was here first. It's about who can make a contribution."

**Sketches and studies of Black's attention to detail of a simple headline.**

# Mad Predictions

*Shots from the Hip*

# Mad Predictions

LINO
TYPE
FACES

Print Lives! They thought the
Internet would kill print.
Wrong: the classics survive.

*The year 2000: the successor to Java runs every electrical appliance you own.*

**—Roger Black**

**B**lack likes to shoot from the hip," says @Home art director John Goecke. With his propensity for prognostication, Black took a few shots at the tin cans of tomorrow.

## Spring 1997
**Personalization**

The inevitable move toward totally custom sites for the viewer takes over the Net.

## Fall 1997
**Transactions**

The primary form of business on the Net explodes as we realize how to hook a customer directly to a product.

## Spring 1998
**Broadband**

There are a million subscribers to cable modem services, which allow rich media, like video, to flow into everyone's homes.

# Fall 1998

## Entertainment

The entertainment mavens notice that when you put video on the screen it seizes all of your attention, and they quickly proclaim the Internet "an entertainment medium." Then comes the rush of big players who threaten to decimate the independent Web we know and love.

# Spring 1999

## Databases

Finally, database technology catches up to the Net. Soon the quality of the database becomes all-important; it becomes understood that this is the only limit on transactions, personalization, and video serving.

# Fall 1999

## A New Medium

We see the first real results of media integration. The Net has enough experience under its belt for producers and creative types to make convincing combinations of multimedia. Finally, the Net moves past being "radio with pictures" and establishes itself as something totally different: a new medium!

 1998: Entertainment attacks the Web

# Spring 2000

## Long Live Print!

Amid the general millennium fever there arises a crisis of confidence. The numerous companies that poured their every last resource into online notice that print did not die. In fact, print is back! But it never really went away. The thing about human nature that thinks new technology kills the old is thwarted again. Radio did not kill theater, television did not kill radio, and the Internet has failed to kill print media. There will be great weeping and gnashing of teeth.

# Fall 2000

## Ubiquity

The Net is now in every room. The successor to Java is running every electrical appliance you own. Bill Gates is nowhere to be seen.

2000: Post-Java appliances

# 2001

## Content

Finally, we realize it *is* all about content. The entire industry realizes that the Internet means nothing without good stories, good personalities, and good direction. Content is king.

2001: None of this matters.

Soon thereafter, a giant monolith is found on the other side of the moon, and, after the expedition to Mars, none of this matters.

# Roger Black 1970–97

*A Visual Biography*

# 1970-71

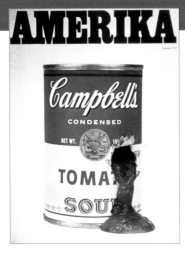

## Print Project: Amerika
Editor

A supplement for college news-papers, *Print Project Amerika* leads Roger Black to drop out of the University of Chicago, but the publication only has one issue. Black, the editor, designs the prototype issue, but lists a friend who helped with the paste-up as art director, "so we'd have more names on the masthead."

## May Day Newspaper
The Amerika team turns to the antiwar demonstration, May Day, in Washington that spring. The plan is to sit in the streets and stop "business as usual" in the nation's capitol.

# 1972

## LA

After a brief stint in a Houston ad agency, Black is hired, at age 23, to be the art director of a new alternative weekly called *LA*. Started by *Newsweek* correspondent Karl Fleming and zillionaire Max Palevsky, the tabloid lasts barely six months. But Black learns to hire staff (chief photographer: David Strick), meet deadlines, and make friends. Also at *LA*, Bill Cardozo, who coined the term *gonzo journalism* and Terry McDonnel, whose path will often cross with Black's over the next twenty years.

PHOTO: TOM INGALLS

**A VISUAL BIOGRAPHY**

# 1975

**Rolling Stone**

Associate Art Director 1975
Art Director 1976-78

Black comes to San Francisco to
work for *Rolling Stone*, with the
assignment from Jann Wenner to
create an original typeface for the

# 1976

magazine. Jim Parkinson designs the type, which is to be introduced over the next three years. In 1976, Black becomes Art Director. Working with such designers as Mary Shanahan, Margery Peters, and Vincent Winter, Black redesigns the magazine gradually. The art department revives classic typefaces and typographical effects (like initial caps, outlines and drop shadows), resulting in a strong retro look that receives the National Magazine Award for design.

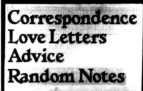

Top: Black's first cover for Rolling Stone. Above and left: Parkinson's early typographical school.

A VISUAL BIOGRAPHY

# 1978-79

**New West**
Design Director

Ex-publisher of *Rolling Stone*, Joe Armstrong, hires Black to design *New West*, the sister publication of *New York*. For a short time Black ran the art departments of both magazines, which were owned by Rupert Murdoch. Staff art directors include Steve Hoffman and Patricia Bradbury. In 1979 Murdoch asks him to do a reworking of the *New York Post*. "It never saw the light of day," says Black, "which may have saved my reputation."

Left: Black with photographer Larry Williams and designer Vincent Winter in 1980.

# 1979-81

**New York**
Design Director

**Los Tiempos Perdidos,
Abel Quezada**
Book Design

**La Historia General,
Sahagún**
Book Design

# 1982-85

**New York Times Magazine**
Art Director, Magazine
Art Director, Editorial Art

Black starts at the *Times* magazine and ultimately succeeds the great newspaper designer Lou Silverstein as chief art director. He still finds time to do freelance work, such as the design of Martha Stewart's first book, *Entertaining*. In 1985 he is approached by *Newsweek's* photo editor, Karen Mullarkey, who had worked with him at *Rolling Stone*. Seeking a quicker pace than offered by the gray lady, Black resigns from *The Times*, which hardly pleases publisher Abe Rosenthal. "I hear you ran from the newsroom," says Ruth Gilbert of *New York* magazine, "followed by an enormous explosion."

# 1982-85

**Eco**
Magazine Project

**American Illustration 4**
Book Design

With the artist Abel Quezada and editor Roger Toll, Black designs *Eco*, a Mexican monthly, using Ventura Publisher and Adobe Illustrator 1.0. With Steve Luciani of *Newsweek* he produces *American Illustration 4* completely electronically.

**Martha Stewart Entertaining**
Book Design, with Patricia Bradbury

**Muppet Magazine**
Launch Design

**Novedades**
Newspaper Redesign, with Mario Garcia

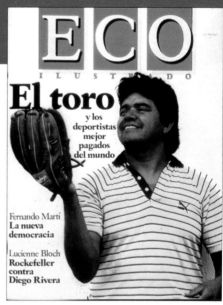

# 1985-86

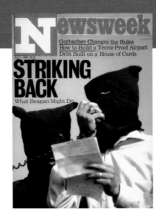

**Newsweek**

Design Director

Magazine Redesign

At the behest of editor Rick Smith, Black introduces a new design, working with deputy art director Patricia Bradbury and designer Martine Winter. As at *Rolling Stone*, Jim Parkinson makes a new typeface, Newsweek NO. 9, based on a 19th-century design. The method developed at *Newsweek* by Smith and Black becomes the basis of Black's redesign method—for publications *and* Web sites.

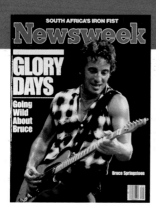

Above: Bruce, before and after redesign.
Below: First redesign cover.

# 1987

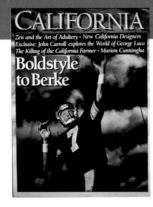

**Roger Black, Incorporated**
President

**Trips**
Magazine Design Art Director

The firm's first client is *Trips,*
an alternative to *National
Geographic* (but the same size),
published by Banana Republic.
The magazine lasts one issue, but
it is the first national magazine
produced entirely on the desktop.
Margery Cantor is art director.

**California**
Magazine Redesign

# 1988

### San Francisco Examiner
Newspaper Redesign

New clients begin to turn to
the desktop, just as they realize
they need a redesign. "We were
scrambling for software. Ready
Set Go, we decided, would work
for *California* magazine." says
Black. "I remember John Miller
learning it in one day, then
training the art department in
L.A., the next.

### Panorama, Italy
Magazine Redesign,
with John Miller

### Type 1987, New York
Conference Chair

### Adobe Systems
Consultant, Type Advisory Board

# 1989

**Más**
Magazine Launch Design

**Smart**
*Magazine Launch Design*
The studio moves to new offices
on Fifth Avenue, shared with a
magazine to be started by Terry
McDonnel, *Smart*. Janet Waegel
and Rhonda Rubenstein become
the art directors. *Smart* is the first
magazine to be produced in color,
entirely on desktop computers.

**Schweitzer Illustrierte,
Switzerland**
Magazine Redesign

**The Font Bureau, Inc., Boston**
Founded with David Berlow

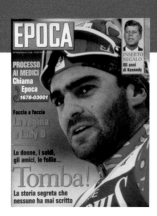

## Roger Black Europe, Srl., Italy
Founded with Sebastiano Castiglioni

"Working abroad, you learn one thing," says Black: "Shed your assumptions. If you don't start at ground zero and learn a culture, the design will never work."

## Hearst Magazines
Design Consultation

## El Sol, Spain
Newspaper Launch Design

## L'Illustré, Switzerland
Magazine Redesign

## Grazia, Italy
Magazine Redesign

## Type90, Oxford
Conference Chair

# 1991

**Zoom, France**
Magazine Redesign

*Zoom* is like a 1970s flashback for Black. "I will never forget riding through the streets of Paris at 3 A.M. on the back of the crazed editor's Harley."

**Toronto Star**
Newspaper Redesign

**Epoca, Italy**
Magazine Redesign

**Chicago Tribune Magazine**
Newspaper Section Redesign

Left: Kristy Brinkley and Black during a cover shoot. Moral: "Never be photographed next to a supermodel with your shirt off."

# 1991

## Esquire
Magazine Redesign

With the collapse of *Smart*, Black quickly moves to Hearst as a consultant to the group's 15 magazines. His client is Claeys Bahrenburg, another *Rolling Stone* alumnus. Terry McDonnel is hired at *Esquire* and the two are working together again, along with art director Rhonda Rubenstein.

225

# 1991-93

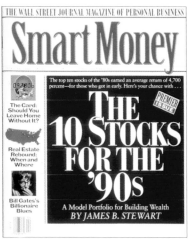

**Smart Money**
Magazine Launch Design

**Il Sabato, Italy**
Magazine Redesign,
with Gerd Malcherek

**Esquire Gentleman**
Magazine Launch Design,
with Maryjane Fahey

**Avui, Spain**
Newspaper Redesign,
with Sebastiano Castiglioni

**Danilo Black, Mexico**
Founded with Eduardo Danilo

# 1993

### Out Magazine
Magazine Design Launch

"*Out* magazine became an opportunity to test our experience at starting magazines on shoestring budgets, using the latest technology," reports Black. "Indeed, we could not have gotten it off the ground without the Macintosh." Michael Goff, the studio's staff editor, leads the effort, and as an intensely-focused niche magazine, *Out* establishes itself quickly and becomes a print prototype for Web sites.

### Time Magazine
Special Issue Design

### Esquire Sportsman
Magazine Launch Design

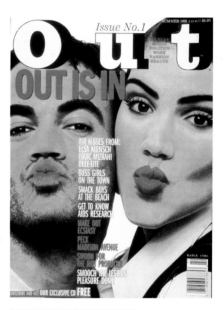

# 1993

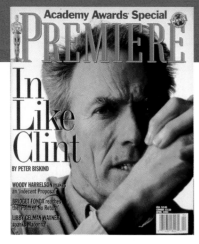

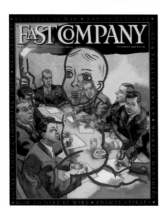

**Premiere**
Magazine Redesign,
with John Schmitz

**Foreign Affairs**
Magazine Redesign,
with Paul Barnes

**Argonaut**
Magazine Launch Design,
with John Miller

**Fast Company**
Magazine Launch Design,
with John Schmitz

**Entrepreneur**
Magazine Redesign

**National Law Journal**
Newspaper Redesign

# 1993

## Esquire
Magazine Redesign

With another change of editors, Black finds himself actually art directing the monthly *Esquire*. It becomes the only magazine he's redesigned twice.

## Information Week
Magazine Redesign

## Gerardo Black Wüllner, Germany
Founded with Gerd Malcherek and Jo Wüllner

## Ferriche Black, Spain
Founded with Ricardo Feriche

# 1994

**Baltimore Sun**
Newspaper Redesign,
with John Goecke

**Placar, Brazil**
Magazine Redesign

"*Placar* was one of those fan-tastic combinations of editorial and publishing ideas coming together at the right moment," says Black. With Thomaz Correa, head of Brazil's Abril magazine group, Black and the design team took an aging soccer magazine with a circula-tion of 50,000 and turned it into one of South America's hottest magazine. Following his slogan, "*Futebol, sexo e rock and roll,*" the magazine now has a circulation of 275,000.

# 1994-95

**Domincal, Spain**
Newspaper Section Launch,
with Ricardo Feriche

**Canadian Living, Canada**
Magazine Redesign,
with Maryjane Fahey

**Crain's New York Business**
Magazine Redesign,
with Maryjane Fahey

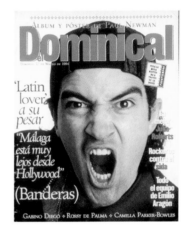

# 1994-95

**Interactive Bureau, New York**

Founded with Jock Spivy
and David Berlow

# 1996

### Discovery Online

Web Site Design Launch,

The Interactive Bureau gets off to a fast start with Discovery Channel Online, produced by an IAB SWAT team lead by Jessica Helfand, working closely with Discovery's art director, John Sanford. While some of the firm's experience in print pays off, it's really a new world, and it was good to get started early. "We weren't on the *Nina* or the *Pinta* or the *Santa Maria*," says Black. "But at least we came over on the *Mayflower*."

# 1996-97

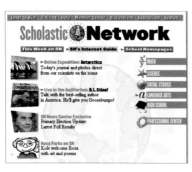

**USA Today Online**
Web Site Design Launch,
with John Schmitz

**American Express**
Intranet Site Design,
with John Schmitz and Theo Fels

**Scholastic Net**
Web Site Redesign,
with John Schmitz

**Snow Country**
Magazine Redesign

**Bristol-Meyers Squibb**
Web Site Design Launch,
with Theo Fells

# 1996-97

**Font Bureau**

Web Site Design Launch,
with David Berlow and Jonathan
Corum

**YPN**

Web Site Design Launch,
with John Schmitz and Steve
Gullo

**@Home Network**

Web Site Design Launch,
with John Goecke

**Barnes & Noble**

Web Site Design Launch,
with Robert Raines

**The Straits Times, Singapore**

Newspaper Redesign,
with Eduardo Danilo

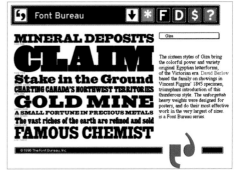

# 1996-97

**Parent Soup**
Web Site Design Launch,
with John Schmitz

**National Park Service**
Web Site Redesign, with John
Miller and Tom Morgan

**Svenska Dagbladet, Sweden**
Newspaper Redesign,
with Michael Jones

**Tages Anzeiger, Switzerland**
Newspaper Redesign,
with Michael Jones

# 1996-97

### @Home Network
Web Site Design Launch,
with John Goecke

### Men's Health
Magazine Redesign,
with Maryjane Fahey

### MSNBC
Web Site Design Launch

# The Typefaces in This Book

Ironically, Bell Gothic was originally designed for phone books. It has a crude, industrial look that was ugly even to the Bell System, which ultimately replaced it with Centennial. In the late 1980s, hip designers were attracted to naive Gothics like Bell and Garage Gothic Regular (used on the cover), which was based on the numbered tickets handed out in parking garages. A whole family of Garage Gothics was designed by Tobias Frere-Jones of the Font Bu-reau. We've used both faces here to contrast with Adobe Jenson. Created by designer Robert Slimbach, Adobe Jenson captures the essence of Nicolas Jenson's roman and Ludovico degli Arrighi's italic designs within an extended typeface family. Adobe Jenson utilizes Adobe's multiple master font technology with two design axes: weight and optical size. Versatility and beauty are combined. The series may be the best of the Adobe originals.

—R.B.